ISBN 978-0-260-38530-7
PIBN 10945198

ESTABLISHED 1794.

E. A. CRUIKSHANK.   WARREN CRUIKSHANK.

E. A. CRUIKSHANK & CO.,

REAL ESTATE,

176 BROADWAY,   NEW YORK.

Entire Charge of Estates taken and the Sale and Rental of
New York City Property a Specialty.

TELEPHONE, NO. 1158 CORTLANDT.

HORACE S. ELY & CO.,

Real Estate Agents,

64 CEDAR ST.,

UPTOWN OFFICE,
27 WEST 30TH STREET,   NEW YORK.
NEAR BROADWAY.

PROMISSORY NOTES

BILLS OF EXCHANGE.
CHECKS AND NEGOTIABLE BONDS

IMPORTANT CHANGES IN THE LAW.

New York Negotiable Instruments Law

WHICH TOOK EFFECT

OCTOBER 1, 1897

ANNOTATED AND INDEXED BY

GEO. W. VAN SICLEN

OF THE NEW YORK BAR.

---

200 Pages; Cloth; Price, $2.00

PUBLISHED BY

RECORD AND GUIDE, 14–16 VESEY STREET

NEW YORK.

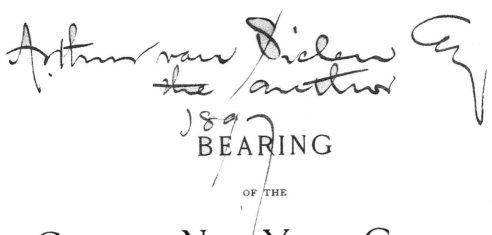

BEARING

OF THE

GREATER NEW YORK CHARTER

UPON

REAL ESTATE INTERESTS.

BY

GEO. W. VAN SICLEN

OF THE NEW YORK BAR.

Author of "Guide to Buyers and Sellers of Real Estate."
Commentaries on "The Negotiable Instruments Law."
Founder of the Title Guarantee and Trust Co.
One of the Incorporators of the Real Estate Exchange.
Sometime Law Editor of The Real Estate Record and Guide.

NEW YORK, 1897.
THE RECORD AND GUIDE PUBLISHING CO.
14-16 VESEY STREET.

Printed by
The Record and Guide Press,
227 William St., N. Y.

Bearing of the Charter

OF

THE CITY OF NEW YORK

UPON

REAL ESTATE INTERESTS

BY

GEO. W. VAN SICLEN

———

Real estate is affected in many ways by provisions of the new charter of New York City, which are scattered and tangled through a law book of over 600 pages; an analysis and summary of these provisions is therefore desirable that they may be clearly understood, and may be quickly found when needed.

Correct name.—The correct name of this great city is not Greater New York, but " The City of New York".

The.—Notice that word "The." It is part of the lawful name of the corporation. Sometimes a charter has that word, and sometimes not, just as the legislature happened (or intended) to pass it; but if it was so written in the charter of a corporation it must be used in all official documents; and if it was not so placed in the charter, it must be left out of all official documents.   In an old law case a person prosecuted for forgery by writing "Nassau Bank," was set free, because the true name of the bank was " *The* Nassau Bank," and he had not written the latter, and consequently had not forged that bank's name.

This is "The City of New York," and not the " City of New York," nor " New York City," when called by its right name.

Short title.—But the charter may be cited by the short title of " The Greater New York Charter".   (Sec. 1.)

Charter takes effect.—The charter takes effect January 1st, 1898, *except* that as to any election required to be held or other act done or forbidden before that date, the new law took effect from and after its passage May 4th, 1897, when it was approved by the Governor.

Not accepted by old New York.—This new charter was accepted by Brooklyn and Long Island City, and not accepted by the old City of New York, but was signed by the Governor, and became a law, notwithstanding.

Rights, powers, obligations, duties.—The new city is declared by Sec. 1 to be the successor corporation in law and fact of all the municipal and public corporations consolidated, with all their rights and powers, and subject to all their lawful obligations; this obviously includes the trustees of each public school district in Hempstead and Flushing, and those of each village in Staten Island and Queens County.

" Developed " or devolved ?—The draftsman of Sec. 1

of the charter evidently believes in the theory of evolution (unless he is misrepresented by the printer), for the law as printed goes on to say that the duties and powers of the several municipal and public corporations consolidated "are hereby *developed* upon the Municipal Assembly of said City of New York." He probably meant "devolved." But in view of the size of the charter and of the way in which it has become, or seemed to become, a law, "developed" is quite a suitable word.

Boroughs.—The five boroughs are Manhattan, The Bronx, Brooklyn, Richmond and Queens.

Former assessments.—All assessments for benefits heretofore laid for the payment of any part of the debts of any of the municipal corporations consolidated, are to be preserved and enforced. (Sec. 5.)

Public buildings and property.—All of the public buildings, institutions, public parks, waterworks and property of the various municipal corporations consolidated, and all the property of the *Counties* of Kings, Richmond and Queens, in the consolidated district (except the Queens County court house and county buildings) become the property of The City of New York on January 1st, 1898. As the county court house of Queens County is in Long Island City, with its court rooms, jail, county treasurer's office, etc., it was evidently thought best to not take that away from the county, only a portion of which is included in the new city of New York.

No more county debts.—After the same date the

Counties of New York, Kings and Richmond cease to have power to become indebted.

No more debts of municipal corporations.—And *after* the same date all the towns, villages, and school districts cease to have power to become indebted. (Sec. 8.) As that power was not taken away by the law until the consummation and taking effect of the consolidation, many of those corporations seized the opportunity to run in debt and bond themselves for large sums, which they never would have authorized or incurred, but for the expectation that the new city will have to foot the bills. Still, they are now parts of the new city, and will have to pay a share; and many needed improvements have been made sooner than they would otherwise have come to pass.

Taxes for 1897.—Each municipal body is to regularly levy its taxes in 1897, as if there were to be no consolidation; and all that are uncollected on January 1st, 1898, will become valid liens due to the new city, and are to be collected by the officers of the new city; the various tax and assessment lists from all the villages and school districts, etc., are to be transmitted to the new comptroller on or immediately after January 1st, 1898, and by him sent to the collector of assessments and arrears for collection. (Sec. 937.)

City Record.—Brief extracts of *all* resolutions and ordinances introduced or passed by the Municipal Assembly, and of all recommendations of committees, and of all final proceedings, and full copies of all messages from the Mayor, and of all reports of departments or officers, are to be published in the City Record immediately after the adjournment of each meeting of the Municipal Assembly. (Sec. 29.) As many of these will affect real estate every one interested will be wise to procure that publication regularly.

Published in City Record.—Every ordinance or resolution providing for the alienation or disposition of any property of the city, the granting of a franchise, terminating the lease of any property or franchise belonging to the city, or the making of any specific improvement, * * * or authorizing * * * the taxing or assessing of property in the city must be published at least five days in the City Record before it can be finally passed by the Municipal Assembly. And the Mayor can not approve it until three days after such publication after its passage. (Sec. 30.)

Keep your City Records on file.—But, note, if an ordinance or resolution (or an abstract of it) has once been published in the City Record, after that it need only be referred to by date and page of the former City Record, stating any amendments.

Real Estate Record and Guide.—A much more convenient method, saving much time, labor, and risk of overlooking important points, will be to subscribe to Real Estate Record and Guide, published weekly at 14–16 Vesey St., in which will be found full reports of everything affecting real estate.

No such resolution or ordinance affecting property can

pass the Council or Board of Aldermen at the same session at which it is offered, except by unanimous consent.

Records and minutes open to inspection.—The City Clerk must keep them open at *all* reasonable times.

City Clerk's signature is necessary to all leases of city property, and all grants and other documents, as under existing laws.   And he keeps the seal.   (Sec. 31.)

Muniments, records, patents, deeds, minutes, writings and papers belonging to the city, and all belonging to the places consolidated, are to be kept by the City Clerk.   (Sec. 32.)

Auctioneers.—Every auctioneer must get a license from the city clerk and file with him a bond for $2,000, with two good sureties.   The President of the Council can revoke the license and forfeit the bond on good cause shown. (Sec. 34.)

Municipal Assembly must meet at least once a month, except in August and September.   (Sec. 37.)

Votes on an assessment, or a franchise.—The votes of three-fourths *of all the members elected* to each house are necessary to the laying of an assessment, or the grant of a franchise.   (Sec. 39.)

Mayor's veto.—The Mayor has to pass on every ordinance and resolution.   He must return it in ten days, or it takes effect.   If he returns it disapproved, it can be passed over his veto by two-thirds of *all the members elected* to each house, unless it involves   *   *   *   the laying of an assessment, or the grant of a franchise, and then it takes five-sixths of all the members elected to each house. (Sec. 40.)

Ordinances in force in 1897 in all the places consolidated are to remain in force within the boundaries of each place, until modified by the Municipal Assembly, and they may be enforced in the name of The City of New York.

Municipal Assembly.—The legislative power of the city is in two houses, the Council and the Board of Aldermen, which taken together constitute the Municipal Assembly.

Council.—There are 29 members of the Council, viz : the President, who is elected on a general ticket just like the Mayor, and 28 members from 10 council districts. Queens County makes one council district, and is to have two members, one from Long Island City and Newtown, and one from Flushing, Jamaica and the part of Hempstead that has been included in the city. Richmond county, the whole of Staten Island, makes another council district, and has two members. The other eight council districts, which have three members each in the council, are shown on the accompanying map.

Ex-Mayors.—Every ex-mayor of The City of New York so long as he remains a resident, is to belong to the Council, but cannot vote in it. Wisdom without power.

Board of Aldermen.—This Board is made up of one representative from each assembly district, except that only one alderman is to be elected by Long Island City and Newtown together, and one by Flushing, Jamaica and the part of Hempstead together ; and also one from the part of the first and second assembly districts of West-chester that have been included in the city.

The President of the Board of Aldermen is elected by them from among their own number.

Heads of departments.—Each head of an administrative department is a member of the Board of Aldermen with the right to talk but not to vote. (Sec. 25.)

The City Clerk is appointed by the Council for six years, so that he holds over longer than the members of the Council, their term being four years, while that of the Aldermen is two.

Additional waterworks may be acquired and constructed by the Municipal Assembly, and the latter is to fix the terms for its distribution. (Sec. 42.)

The height of buildings may hereafter be restricted by the Municipal Assembly, but such an ordinance must first be approved by the Board of Public Improvements; and it needs a majority of *all the members elected*, in each house to pass it, the vote being taken by ayes and noes. (Sec. 43.)

Franchises for street railways and ferries and ferry leases may be granted by the Municipal Assembly. (Sec. 45.)

Where ordinances, rules and regulations originate.—Any *modification* of the existing rules, regulations and ordinances affecting any of the departments (Health, Police, Park, Fire and Building Departments), and all ordinances to be passed to govern the Board of Public Improvements *must originate with the department concerned*, and must be adopted or rejected by the Municipal Assembly *without amendment*. But except where the power to make *new* rules, regulations and ordinances is *expressly conferred* on a department, the power to do so is in the Municipal Assembly; and so is the power to *repeal* them. (Sec. 47.)

Markets, parks, parkways, boulevards, driveways, bridges, ferries, tunnels under streams only, docks, wharves, piers—acquiring land for said purposes, public buildings, school houses, sites therefor.—The power to provide by ordinance for all these is in the Municipal Assembly. (Sec. 48.) So is the power to

Regulate the use of streets, highways, roads, public places and sidewalks; and the temporary occupation of them for erecting and repairing a building on an adjoining lot; and the erection of *booths* and *stands within stoop lines,* but only for the sale of *newspapers, periodicals, fruits* and *soda water,* and only with the *consent of the adjoining owner.* (Sec. 49.)

Regulate the opening of street surfaces; the numbering of houses, and naming of streets (but you can't change a number or a name between May 1st and December 1st); the use of streets and sidewalks for signs, sign-posts, awnings, awning-posts, horse troughs, urinals, telegraph posts and other purposes. To regulate pavements, cross-walks, curbs, gutters, sidewalks; and *banners* or placards or flags across streets, or from houses or other buildings; and advertisements, or hand-bills along the streets; and in relation to public fountains; and to places of public amusement; also to vaults, cisterns, areas, hydrants, sewers and pumps; and partition walls and fences; also in relation to bone boiling, fat rendering and other noxious businesses.

To regulate the *fees for searches* and certificates to be charged *by the collector of assessments and arrears.*

For all these you must apply to the Municipal Assembly, or to the ordinances which it may enact to regulate them, as it has the power under Sec. 49.

Court houses.—Many court rooms are needed not only for the courts of record, but for the city magistrates and police justices all over the city. It takes two-thirds of *all the members elected* to each house to pass a resolution assigning any such place. (Sec. 53.)

Commissioners of deeds are to be appointed by the *Board of Aldermen* alone. (Sec. 58.)

Franchises can only be granted by *ordinance.* (Sec. 72.)

Inalienable.—The rights of the city in and to its water front, ferries, wharf property, land under water, public landings, wharves, docks, streets, avenues, parks, and all other public places are *inalienable;* they can not hereafter be sold nor given nor granted away. (Sec. 71.)

No franchise for more than twenty-five years can be granted hereafter to use streets, avenues, parkways or highways; but it may contain a clause for *renewals* for not more than twenty-five years all told at fair re-valuations; and may provide for the "plant" to become the property of the city at the end of the franchise without

,further compensation to the grantee ; or that the city may buy it at a fair valuation [leaving out the value of the franchise]. (Sec. 73.)

Before granting a franchise to use any street, avenue, parkway or highway, the whole grant, with rates, fares and charges must be published twenty days, and it must be voted for by at least three-fourths of all the members elected to each branch of the Municipal Assembly and approved by the Mayor ; it takes a vote of five-sixths of all the members elected to each branch to pass such a grant for renewal or extension over his veto. (Sec. 74.)*

Old buildings and parcels of land no longer needed for public use may be disposed of by the city, on approval by the Sinking Fund Commissioners, at public sale.

Grants to city of lands under water.—The city has control of the water front of the entire city (subject to the rights of private owners of property) and power to acquire and construct wharves and docks and everything necessary or proper in aid of commerce. And the charter grants in fee to the city all the rights of the State of New York to any and all lands under water in all the rivers and waters in and around the city, and the right to fill in. (Sec. 83.) And the city can not sell any of this property, but must

[*NOTE.—*Sec.* 77 *of the Charter says that Section* 93 *of Chapter* 565 *of the Laws of* 1890, *and amendments thereto, shall not apply to grants under this title. That Chapter* 565 *is the General Railroad Law of the State, and Sec.* 93 *relates to the sale at auction, to the highest bidder, of the franchise to use any street, avenue or park for a railroad. As before stated, this is not to apply to the new city of New York.*]

hold it all *in perpetuity*.   But the city can lease it from time to time, like other property.   (Sec. 84.)

Private rights of owners of shore property, docks and piers, could not be, and are not, taken away by this grant to the city.   (Sec. 85.)

No patent of land under water can hereafter be granted except to the city, or to the riparian proprietor (of the adjoining upland.)   If the city wants it, compensation must be made to the riparian proprietor for his rights.   All such matters in each case may be judicially determined in an action in court brought by the city.   (Sec. 86.)

Mayor.—The *executive* power of The City of New York is vested in the Mayor, as chief executive, and in the officers of the departments.   The Mayor can not be re-elected for the *next* term after the expiration of his term. (Sec. 94.)

Administrative departments.—There are eighteen administrative departments ; six of them being represented in the Board of Public Improvements.   As directly or indirectly real estate interests are affected by each of them, we will enumerate them as they are stated in Sec. 96 of the charter.

Department of Finance.

Law Department.

Police Department.

Represented in the Board of Public Improvements :

    1. Department of Water Supply.

    2. Department of Highways.

3. Department of Street Cleaning.
4. Department of Sewers.
5. Department of Public Buildings, Lighting and Supplies.
6. Department of Bridges.

Department of Parks.
Department of Buildings.
Department of Public Charities.
Department of Correction.
Fire Department.
Department of Docks and Ferries.
Department of Taxes and Assessments.
Department of Education.
Department of Health.

The Comptroller is the head of the Department of Finance.

The Corporation Counsel is the head of the Law Department.

The Police Board of four Police Commissioners constitutes the head of the Police Department. There are over 7,000 policemen.

The President of the Board of Public Improvements is the head of that Board.

The Commissioner of Water Supply is the head of that department.

The Commissioner of Highways,

The Commissioner of Street Cleaning,

The Commissioner of Sewers, with 700 miles of sewers in charge,

The Commissioner of Public Buildings, Lighting and Supplies, and

The Commissioner of Bridges are the heads of those departments, respectively. (Sec. 100.)

The Park Board, consisting of three Commissioners of Parks, constitutes the head of the Department of Parks. There are about 5,000 acres of parks.

The Board of Buildings, consisting of three Commis-sioners of Buildings, constitutes the head of the Depart-ment of Buildings. There are about 170,000 dwellings, churches, and business houses.

The Board of Public Charities, consisting of three com-missioners of charities, constitute the head of that depart-ment.

The Commissioner of Correction is the head of that de-partment.

The Fire Commissioner is the head of the Fire Depart-ment. There are over 2,000 paid firemen.

The Board of Docks, consisting of three commissioners of docks, constitutes the head of the Department of Docks and Ferries. There are 75 miles of wharfage.

The Board of Taxes and Assessments, consisting of a president and four other commissioners of taxes and assess-ments, constitutes the head of that department.

The Board of Education, consisting of nineteen mem-bers, constitutes the head of the Department of Education.

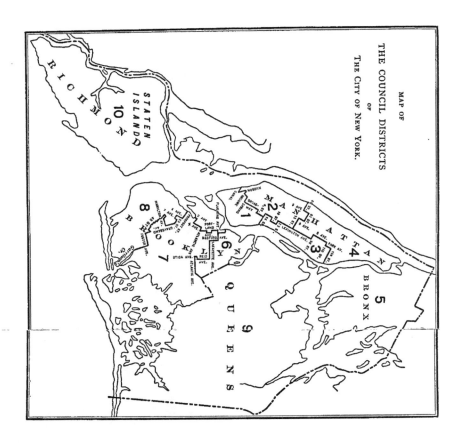

MAP OF
THE COUNCIL DISTRICTS
OF
THE CITY OF NEW YORK.

The (

in charg

The (

Supplie

The (

departr

The l

Parks,

There :

The

sioners

ment (

church

The

missio

ment.

The

partm(

The

ment.

The

of doc

and F

The

presid

ments

The

bers, (

The Board of Health, consisting of the President of the Police Board, the Health Officer of the port, and three Health Commissioners, constitutes the head of the Health Department. (Sec. 109.)

Erection or repair of any city building is to be superintended by a board or commission the members of which are to be appointed by the Mayor. (Sec. 118.)

Any lease of property leased to the city, authorized by the Commissioners of the Sinking Fund, shall be entered into by the *Comptroller.*

The assent of the Comptroller shall be necessary to all agreements made by any city officer or department *for the purchase of any real estate* or easement therein that involves payment by the city ; and the Comptroller must have thirty days' notice of every confirmation of an award requiring the city to pay for acquiring real estate for the city.

Bureaus of the Finance Department; of these there shall be five :

1. One for management of the markets, and collection of rents, interest and revenue, to be known as the *Bureau for the Collection of City Revenue and Markets.*

2. *The Bureau for the Collection of Taxes,* whose chief officer is the Receiver of Taxes.

3. *The Bureau for Collection of Assessments* and Arrears.

4. *The Auditing Bureau.*

5. The *Bureau* for receiving and taking care of the city's money and for payment of the Comptroller's warrants, the chief officer of which is the *Chamberlain.*

2

The bonds of the Receiver of Taxes, and the Collector of Assessments and Arrears, to the amount of $25,000 each, are liens on their real estate and that of their bondsmen, respectively. (Sec. 152.)

Offices for receipt of taxes and assessments are to be in each borough, Brooklyn, The Bronx, Manhattan, Queens and Richmond ; and all taxes, assessments and arrears on property in each borough are to be paid at those respective offices. (Sec. 157.)

Assessment lists are to be filed in the Comptroller's office, all of them in detail, with the date of confirmation and the date of entry in such record. (Sec. 159.)

An assessment becomes a lien immediately upon its entry in that record *in the Comptroller's office*. If the property is in any other borough than Manhattan, *a copy* of the list is to be filed in the office of the collector of assessments for that borough. (But remember, it is a lien from the time the original is filed in the Comptroller's office.) A list for the borough of Manhattan is not copied, but stays there in the Comptroller's office. (Sec. 159.)

Markets, for farmers and market-gardeners, and a general market, are set apart at Gansevoort and Washington streets and Tenth and Thirteenth avenues by Sec. 163.

Bonds for ten dollars each can be issued by The City of New York, and preference is to be given to applicants for the smallest amounts and smallest denominations of bonds, hereafter. (Sec. 171.)

City property, how sold or leased.—The Commissioners

of the Sinking Fund have the power to sell or lease, for the highest price, or rent, at auction or by sealed bids, only after advertisement and appraisal, any city property (except parks, wharves, piers, and land under water) : no lease to be for more than ten years, and with one renewal of not more than ten years.

Market property (except Sixteenth street and Avenue C, Gouverneur Slip and Old Slip markets) can only be sold or leased for markets. (Sec. 205.)

Sinking Fund.—The Sinking Fund of The City of New York is created by Secs. 206 to 216.

Leases to the city, for use by the city for its purposes, must be first presented to the Sinking Fund Commissioners, upon a report of the Comptroller of all the facts relating to such piece of property and his opinion in regard to the proposed lease. (Sec. 217.)

Lands may be ceded to U. S. Government to improve Harlem River by the Commissioners of the Sinking Fund, or by the Municipal Assembly ; that is, all the estate, right, title, and interest of The City of New York in such lands as may be required for that purpose. (Sec. 218.) The lands in this city now owned by the United States Government are worth over $30,000,000.

School buildings and lots no longer needed for school purposes may be sold at auction by the Sinking Fund Commissioners, upon application of the Board of Education. (Sec. 220.) There are over 300 school buildings, and over 200,000 scholars, with 7,500 teachers.

Taxes when Sinking Fund is not sufficient to meet bonds falling due may be increased to an amount sufficient to pay the bonds off. (Sec. 228.) It is to be hoped that this power will be used wisely, and that bonds falling due will be extended or renewed, and that posterity may be called on to share some of the hundreds of permanent improvements, rather than that we of to-day should have *too* high a tax rate.

Taxes are levied and raised under Sections 247, 248 and 249. The Comptroller submits an estimate to the Municipal Assembly four weeks before its annual meeting, for the purpose of levying the taxes. The Municipal Assembly fixes the amount, and then adds "for deficiencies" not over three per cent. of the aggregate amount. The total is about $70,000,000 every year. It will increase.

Corporation Counsel.—All legal proceedings in opening, widening, altering and closing streets, and in acquiring real estate for the city by condemnation proceedings, and the preparation of all leases, deeds, contracts, bonds, and other legal papers of the city or any department, shall be in charge of and conducted by the Corporation Counsel, and he shall approve as to form all such contracts, leases, deeds, bonds and other legal papers. (Sec. 255.)

A **Bureau of Street Opening,**

A **Bureau for Recovery of Penalties,**

A **Bureau for Collection of Arrears of Personal Taxes,** are to be established by the Corporation Counsel, with such other bureaus as he may deem necessary. (Secs. 258 to 260.)

Claims against the city can not be sued for unless the demand or claim was presented to the Comptroller at least *thirty days before* the suit is begun, and he refused or neglected to adjust or pay it. (Sec. 261.)

Supreme Court has exclusive jurisdiction of all actions against the city. (Sec. 262.)

The Police Department of the new city is governed by Secs. 270 to 371. It has been made too powerful. In the course of time the citizens are likely to lose their individuality and their rights.

The Police Department is to co-operate with the Board of Health, and policemen are to arrest for violation of the rules of the Board of Health. (Secs. 310, 311.) This affects real estate owners, because many of the ordinances and rules of the latter Board relate to *Tenement* and *Lodging Houses*, Secs. 1304 to 1325, as well as to Nuisances, Secs. 1287 to 1298, and to other similar matters.

Steam boilers must be inspected by the police annually. (Sec. 342.)

Boroughs.—Each of the five boroughs has its own *President*, elected in his own borough, at the same election with the Mayor of the city, and holding his office four years. (Sec. 382.) He is a member of the local board of every district of local improvements in his borough. (Sec. 383.) And calls all meetings of the various local boards ; and certifies all resolutions, proceedings and determinations of the local boards of local improvements in his borough. (Sec. 384.)

Districts of Local Improvements.—There are twenty-two such districts, corresponding in boundaries to the existing senatorial districts situated in whole or in part within The City of New York. They are to be named or numbered by the Municipal Assembly after January 1st, 1898. (Sec. 390.)

The Local Board is in each district of local improvements; its jurisdiction is confined to those subjects or matters, in its own district, the costs and expenses of which are in whole or in part a charge upon the people or property of that district or of a part of it. The Local Board consists of the president of the borough and of each member of the Municipal Assembly who is a resident of such local improvement district, (and if he moves out of the district he ceases to be a member of that local board).

The charter does not explicitly say so, but it is probably true that if he moves into another local improvement district he becomes at once a member of the local board of the latter.

If any of the local improvements over which a local board has power happen to be in more than one local improvement district, the members of the local boards in all the districts which the improvement affects, together constitute the local board for that particular improvement. (Sec. 391.)

Powers of a local board.—A local board shall have

power in all cases where the cost of improvement is to be met in whole or in part by assessments upon the property benefited, to recommend that proceedings be initiated to open, close, extend, widen, grade, pave, regrade, repave, and repair streets, avenues and public places, and to construct lateral sewers within the district; to flag or reflag, curb or recurb sidewalks, to relay cross-walks, to set or reset lamps, and to provide signs designating names of streets.

A local board has a few other powers, to listen to complaints and to pass resolutions.   (Sec. 393.)

Meetings of each local board shall be held in the main hall or public building of the borough, whenever called by the president.

A **quorum of a local board** is constituted by the president and one other member.   (Sec. 394.)

Local improvement.   How bring it about.

Send in a petition to the president of the borough.

He must appoint a time for a meeting of the proper local board, not more than fifteen days thereafter.

He must publish in the "City Record," at least ten days before that meeting, a notice when it will be held, and that the petition is on file in his office for inspection.   (Sec. 400.)

Then the local board, after consideration of the petition, may recommend that proceedings be initiated to open, to close, to extend, to widen, to regulate, to grade, to curb, to gutter, to flag, and to pave streets, to lay crosswalks, and to construct lateral sewers within its district, and generally

for such other improvements in and about such streets as
the public wants and convenience of the district shall require.   (Sec. 401.)

Then the local board shall forthwith transmit a copy
of its resolution recommending the improvement, to the
Board of Public Improvements (see page 23, *post*) and if
the latter board thinks it ought to be proceeded with, it
shall go on with it in the regular routine of said Board of
Public Improvements.   (See 413 to 422, pages 23 to 26, *post*.)

The expense of all such improvements shall be assessed,
and be a lien on the property benefited *in proportion to the
amount of benefit*, and in no case shall extend beyond the
limits of said district.   (Sec. 402.)

The local board has power, apparently *without petition*,
to cause the flagging or reflagging of sidewalks, laying or
relaying of crosswalks, fencing vacant lots, digging down
lots or filling in sunken lots within its district, by resolution approved by the Board of Public Improvements.   After
such public work or improvement is authorized, the Board
of Public Improvements attends to it and goes ahead with
it, as in case of similar work authorized after petition.
(See Secs. 413 to 422, pages 23 to 26, *post.*)

But the Board of Public Improvements has power to order
and authorize any of these local improvements without
action by the local board.

And no local board can incur any expenditures (by The
City of New York) other than as authorized by the Board
of Estimate and Apportionment.   (Sec. 404.)

Board of Public Improvements.—This board is constituted by combining the Mayor, Corporation Counsel, Comptroller, the commissioners of water supply, highways, street cleaning, sewers, public buildings, lighting and supplies, and bridges, and the presidents of the boroughs, together with a President of the Board of Public Improvements (appointed by the Mayor), seventeen in all; but the Mayor, Corporation Counsel, Comptroller and borough presidents don't count in making up a quorum; and a Borough President cannot vote except upon matters relating exclusively to his own borough. (Sec. 410.) A majority of the remaining nine members, that is five, constitute a quorum. This board must meet at least once a week. (Sec. 412.)

Any public work in the department of any commissioner who is a member of this board, that may be the subject of a contract, must first be approved by this Board of Public Improvements, and by the Municipal Assembly.

No work involving assessment for benefit, shall be authorized by the Board of Public Improvements until there has been submitted to it a written estimate of the cost and the assessed value, on the last tax-roll, of the real estate to be assessed. (Sec. 413.)

The Municipal Assembly can not enter directly into any contract whatever for any public work or improvement. There must first be a report by the Board of Public Improvements; and if that be unfavorable, it takes a vote of five-sixths of both houses, and the Mayor's approval, to pass it. (Sec. 414.)

Powers of Board of Public Improvements:

1. Adoption of a map or plan for any part of the city not yet mapped.

2. Acquiring title to land for parks, streets, bridges, and tunnels.

3. Acquiring title to land for sewers.

4. Approval of plans for sewerage and drainage.

5. Construction, repairing and cleaning sewers and drains.

6. Repairs of pavements and readjusting grades of streets in connection therewith.

7. Water rents and contracts for water supply with private companies or other municipalities.

8. Any public work provided for in the tax levy or by issue of bonds. But in issuing bonds for repairing streets, the *Municipal Assembly* can designate the boroughs where the money is to be expended. (Sec. 415.)

Ordinances to be prepared by Board of Public Improvements.—This board has to prepare and recommend to the Municipal Assembly all ordinances regulating many matters which affect real estate, as follows:

1. Laying water pipes; making all attachments thereto, and *extending, constructing*, and repairing *the waterworks*.

2. Regulating, grading, curbing, guttering, flagging and paving streets, laying crosswalks, constructing, reconstructing and repairing streets, making all excavations in streets for public purposes, prescribing width of sidewalks, and regulating manner of constructing and laying sidewalks.

3. Encroachments upon and obstructions in the streets, and authorizing and requiring their removal.

4. The use of streets and sidewalks for signs, sign-posts, awnings, awning-posts, horse-troughs, urinals, telegraph-posts and other purposes.

5. The exhibition of handbills or advertisements along the streets.

6. Construction, repair and use of vaults, cisterns, areas, hydrants and pumps.

7. Construction and repair of public markets.

8. Preservation and protection of any and all of the waterworks, to ensure pure and wholesome water.

9. Cleaning and sprinkling streets, and the use of streets and sidewalks for building purposes, and *for all other* temporary or *business purposes.*

10. Laying gas pipes, electric wires, steam pipes, pneumatic tubes ; and lighting all public places and streets ; and inspecting gas or electricity and meters for both, and all electric wires ; and the opening of streets to lay pipes, wires and tubes.

11. Erecting, extending and repairing public buildings (other than school houses, alms houses, penitentiaries, and police and fire station houses).

12. The rates of fare on the Brooklyn Bridge, and on any other bridges.

13. Making all contracts for public work or supplies. (Sec. 416.)

Rules and plans may be prescribed by the Board of Public Improvements for regulating, grading, curbing, guttering, also for crosswalks and sidewalks *throughout the city*. (Sec. 418.)

Every piece of work or job, the several parts of which cost together over $1,000, must be by contract established by ordinance or resolution of the Municipal Assembly, and advertised in the City Record, and awarded to the lowest bidder. However, the head of a department may reject all bids. And a majority of the Board of Public Improvements of whom the Mayor and Comptroller shall be two, may award a contract to a bidder not the lowest. (Sec. 419.)

Assessments for local improvements are laid as directed by Sec. 422.

Comptroller is to pay contractors as directed in Sec. 423.

No contractor can be let off from a fine or penalty, nor can his *time be extended*, except by the *unanimous* vote of the Board of Public Improvements. (Sec. 424.)

The maps or plans of the old city, and of the 23rd and 24th wards, and of Brooklyn and Long Island City, heretofore laid out and adopted as permanent, shall remain the maps or plans of the new city so far as they cover its territory, and be deemed final and conclusive as to *location, width and grade of streets* (so far as heretofore adopted). (Sec. 432.)

Map is to be completed by the President of the Board of Public Improvements as required by Sec. 433. And if he is slow about it he may be *required* to complete the whole or any part within a fixed time. (Sec. 434.)

Whenever any street in The City of New York *shall have been used* as such for upwards *of twenty years* without having its grade established by law, *the* level or *surface of such street as so used* shall be deemed to be and to have been the grade thereof. (Sec. 433.)

This section is going to make trouble. Some will claim that it cannot be used for twenty years as a street in " The City of New York " before the arrival of January 1st, 1918. But others will claim, and probably successfully, that some old streets were streets before there was any new city called " The City of New York," and they came into the new city on January 1st, 1898, as streets already, and as streets twenty years old, but without any grade *established by law*. However, the

Grade may be changed and so may the map or plan of the city, under Sec. 436. But, of course, such alterations will often bring great expense upon the city.

Maps and plans are to be filed, and maps and profiles showing changes, one in the Register's office, one in the Corporation Counsel's office, and one in the office of the Board of Public Improvements. (Sec. 437.) So are

Drainage plans, in the same offices (Sec. 439), after the drainage and sewer system are completed, as directed by Sec. 438.

The grade of a street may be raised for proper drainage. (Sec. 441.)

Main Offices of the Departments of Water Supply, Highways, Street Cleaning, Sewers, Public Buildings, Lighting and Supplies, and Bridges, shall be in the borough of Manhattan. There *may* be branch offices with deputy commissioners in the other boroughs, when appointed by the commissioner of any department. (Sec. 452.)

"Street."—The word "street" or "streets" in this charter includes "street, avenue, road, alley, lane, highway, boulevard, concourse, public square and public place," or the plurals thereof respectively. (Sec. 462.)

Water supply.—There are 325,000,000 gallons of water consumed daily, or 100 gallons to every man, woman and child. The Department of Water Supply is under a commissioner of water supply, who has control :

1. Of all structures and property connected with that supply, including fire and drinking hydrants and water meters.

2. Of maintaining the quality of the water, and of the construction of works necessary to deliver it.

3. Of collection of water rents.

4. Of enforcing regulations concerning its use. (Sec. 469.)

The Department of Water Supply is governed by the rules laid down in Title 4, Secs. 468 to 517 of the charter.

Water rents are fixed by the Municipal Assembly. (Sec. 473.)

Meters are governed as directed by Sec. 475.

Proceedings to acquire title to real estate needed for water supply must be taken under Secs. 484 to 508.

" Real estate " defined. As used in this chapter (that is, chapter X. of the charter, which relates to the Board of Public Improvements, and comprises Secs. 410 to 601,) the term "real estate" shall be construed to signify and embrace all uplands, lands under water, the water of any lake, pond or stream, all water rights or privileges, and any and all easements and hereditaments, corporeal and incorporeal, and every estate, interest and right, legal and equitable, in lands or water, or any privilege or easement thereunder, including terms for years, and liens thereon by way of judgment, mortgages or otherwise, and also all claims for damage to such real estate. It shall also be construed to include all real estate (as the term is above defined) heretofore acquired or used for railroad, highway or other purpose, (providing the persons or corporations owning such real estate, or claiming interest therein, shall be allowed the perpetual use, for such purposes, of the same or of such other real estate to be acquired for the purposes of this act as will afford practicable route or location for such railroad, highway or other public purpose, and in the case of a railroad commensurate with and adapted to its needs ; and provided, also, that such persons or corporations shall not, directly or indirectly, be subject to expense, loss or damage by reason of changing such route or location, but that such expense, loss or damage shall be borne by the city.) (Sec. 484.)

This is a pretty good, broad definition of real estate. Evidently water is sometimes real estate ; in fact the ancient legal maxim is *"Aqua cedit solo,"* water belongs to or goes with the land. You can't bring a suit to recover possession of a lake, or of *water* only, but you must bring it for the *land* that lies at the bottom, and call it *land covered with water*. A right to fish (called in law the right of piscary) and a mill right, or right to use the overflow from a dam, are examples of water rights and privileges.

An easement is a liberty, privilege, or advantage in land, without profit, existing distinct from an ownership of soil; thus the right to use a public highway is a public easement; and the right to use a gateway, or a right of way for one family over another's land, is a private easement.

A **hereditament is** anything that may be inherited; everything that goes to an heir (it really includes every kind of interest in real estate); a piece of furniture which is an heirloom, and which by custom descends to the heir together with a house, is a hereditament. And so is the house.

A **corporeal hereditament** is of a material nature; you can perceive it by your senses; *land* is a corporeal hereditament.

An incorporeal hereditament is one that is not perceived by the bodily senses, such as a right of way in a lane, or a right to pasture cattle on a common.

An estate is the condition or circumstance in which the owner stands with regard to his property; it is the same

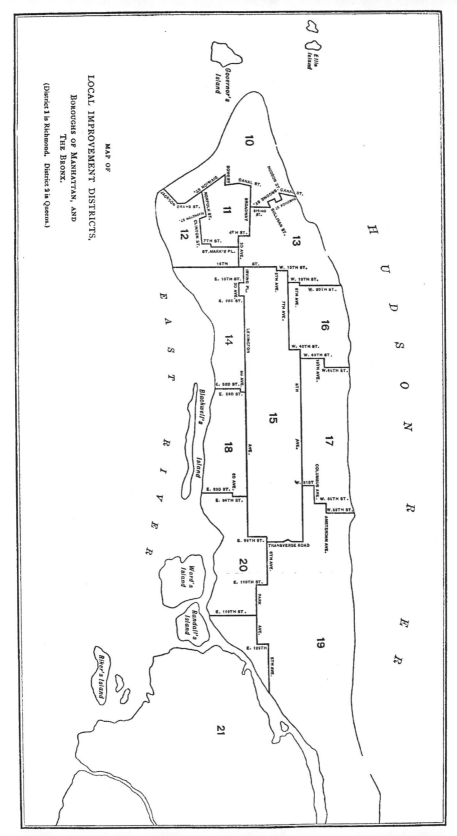

MAP OF
LOCAL IMPROVEMENT DISTRICTS,
BOROUGHS OF MANHATTAN, AND
THE BRONX.
(District 1 is Richmond. District 2 is Queens.)

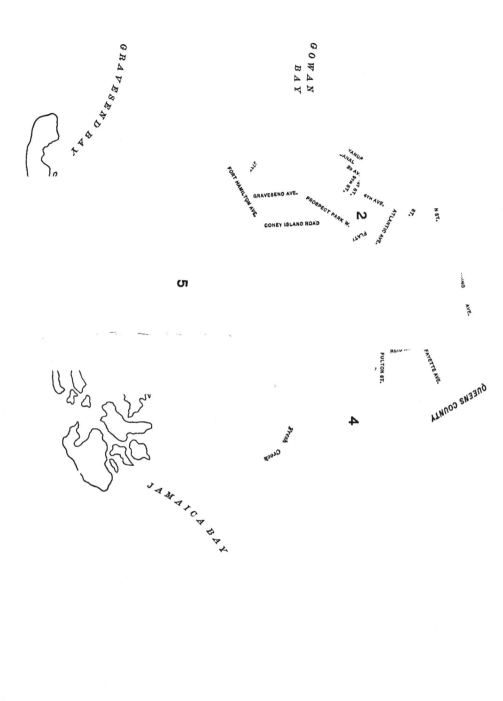

GRAVESEND BAY

GOWAN
BAY

FORT HAMILTON AVE.

GRAVESEND AVE.

CONEY ISLAND ROAD

PROSPECT PARK W.

VANUP
ANAL
20 AV.
9TH ST.
1ST ST.
4TH AVE.

ATLANTIC AVE.

FLATT

2

ST.

N ST.

5

...ING

AVE.

REID A...

FULTON ST.

FAYETTE AVE.

QUEENS COUNTY

4

Creek

JAMAICA BAY

as "right, title and interest" in property ; it may be an estate of inheritance, or an estate in fee simple, or an estate for life, or an estate by the curtesy (which is the husband's right to the income of his wife's property so long as he lives after her death, if she made no will, and if they ever had a child born *alive*), or an estate for years, etc., etc.

A **legal estate** is that kind of estate of which the *courts of common law* will take cognizance, such as an estate in fee simple in an ejectment suit.

An equitable estate is one acquired by the *operation of equity*, such as the estate or title of a ward for whose use lands are held in trust by a trustee who holds the *legal* estate (that is the deed or title to the lands being in the trustee's name.)

A **term for years** is a *limited* period of time for which an estate is granted, as under a lease ; it is called a *term* because it has a certain beginning and a certain end.

The other words and phrases in this definition of "real estate" in Sec. 485 explain themselves. But all the foregoing terms, and many others, are fully explained in **Van Siclen's Guide to Buyers and Sellers of Real Estate, and New York Real Property Law,** published by the **Record and Guide,** 14 and 16 Vesey St., New York.

There are about 360 square miles of land in the new city limits, and it is assessed at about $2,400,000,000, so that it is fairly worth over $4,000,000,000.

The head of the Department of Highways is the Com-

3

missioner of Highways. He shall have cognizance and
control of

1. Regulating, grading, curbing, flagging and guttering
streets, and laying crosswalks.

2. Constructing and repairing public roads.

3. Paving, repaving, resurfacing and repairing all streets ;
and relaying all pavements *removed for any cause.*

4. Laying or relaying surface railroad tracks, form of
rail, etc.

5. Filling sunken lots, fencing vacant lots, digging down
lots, and licensing vaults under sidewalks.

6. Recommending ordinances relating to his department.

7. Removal of incumbrances.

8. Issue of permits to builders and others to use the
streets, but not to open them.   (Sec. 524.)

A **permit from Department of Highways** is necessary
before there can be any removal of the pavement or dis-
turbance of the surface of any street for vaults, cellars,
buildings, sewers, water, gas, electric wires, or any purpose
whatever. And it must be relaid promptly and to the
satisfaction of the commissioner, or he can have it done
over again, after notice to you, and the cost will be a lien
on the property like an assessment.   (Sec. 525.)

**Office of Commissioner of Street Improvements in
23rd and 24th wards** is abolished.   The Commissioner
of Highways of The City of New York will have all his
powers and duties hereafter.   (Sec. 526.)   And so will the
latter administer in former Brooklyn, Long Island City

Richmond County, and part of the County of Queens, all the powers and duties in relation to regulating, grading, curbing, guttering, paving, laying crosswalks, and filling lots, that were exercised heretofore by the municipal corporation of each of said cities, and of each town and village in each of said counties. (Sec. 527.)

The Department of Street Cleaning besides the ordinary and usual duties of such a department, has powers which affect the rights of each individual owner of real estate, as laid down in subdivision 2, Sec. 534, viz. : cognizance and control

"2. Of the framing of regulations controlling the use of sidewalks and gutters by abutting owners and occupants for the disposition of sweepings, garbage, etc., which regulations shall have the force of city ordinances, and shall be enforced by the police."

Private sewers may be constructed in city streets, on approval by the Commissioner of Sewers and the Board of Public Improvements, under the rules laid down in Sec. 560.

The Commissioner of Sewers succeeds to the powers and duties, in his department, of the old corporations of the various cities, towns and villages consolidated, including those of the former Commissioner of Street Improvements in the 23rd and 24th wards. (Secs. 565, 566.)

Public baths and public urinals are to be cared for, managed and maintained by the Department of Public Buildings, Lighting and Supplies.

Testing gas, and gas meters, and electric meters and

electric lights, and meters for steam furnished for use to any person are all in charge of the Commissioner of Public Buildings, Lighting and Supplies hereafter. (Sec. 575.)

The transmission of electricity, gas, steam, and pneumatic power, in, or through any and all streets and public places, is under the control of said Commissioner of Public Buildings, Lighting and Supplies. (Sec. 573, subdivision 2.)

Separate contracts for lighting each borough are to be made by the commissioner. (Sec. 587.)

Park Commissioners are to be appointed to have administrative jurisdiction, one in the boroughs of Manhattan and Richmond, one in the borough of The Bronx, and one in the boroughs of Brooklyn and Queens. (Sec. 607.)

The head of the Department of Buildings is to be called the **Board of Buildings,** which will consist of three **commissioners of buildings;** one is to be appointed to have administrative jurisdiction in the boroughs of Manhattan and The Bronx, one in the borough of Brooklyn, and one in the boroughs of Queens and Richmond. (Sec. 644.)

Each commissioner succeeds to the powers and duties of the Department of Buildings, or Superintendent of Buildings, whose place he takes. (Sec. 646.)

The Board of Buildings can make new rules and regulations. (Sec. 645.)

Present laws and rules for construction, alteration or removal of buildings continue in force in   borough or locality until new rules are made by the Board of Buildings.

A "**Building Code**" is to be provided by the Municipal Assembly, and when established is to take the place of the existing laws. (Sec. 647.)

The present building law, and regulations of the building department, are found in their most convenient and intelligible form, fully analyzed and indexed by Mr. William J. Fryer, in the volume published in 1897 by The Record and Guide, 14–16 Vesey Street, New York : "Laws Relating to Buildings in New York City." This valuable treatise contains :

I. The Building Law.

II. Law Limiting Heights of Dwelling Houses. Law Requiring Temporary Floorings.

III. Regulations of the Building Department.

IV. Tenement and Lodging House Laws.

V. Regulations of the Department of Public Works.

VI. Revised Ordinances of the City Pertaining to Buildings.

VII. Laws Relating to Extinction and Prevention of Fires, and to Explosives and Combustibles in Buildings.

VIII. State Factory Inspection Law.

IX. Mechanics' Lien Law of 1897.

The completeness of this treatise requires that the exact text of the new charter in relation to the Department of Buildings should be included here. It is as follows:

CHAPTER XII.
DEPARTMENT OF BUILDINGS.

Appointment of commissioners; qualifications; juris-diction; salaries.—Sec. 644. The head of the department of buildings shall be called the board of buildings. Said board shall consist of three members to be known as commissioners of buildings. They shall be appointed by the mayor and shall hold their respective offices as provided in chapter IV. of this act. Each of said commissioners shall be a competent architect or builder of at least ten years' experience. One of said commissioners shall be the president of the board, and shall be so designated by the mayor. In appointing such commissioners the mayor shall specify the borough or boroughs in which they are respectively to have administrative jurisdiction, to wit: One in the boroughs of Manhattan and the Bronx; one in the borough of Brooklyn, and one in the boroughs of Queens and Richmond. The principal office of the department of buildings shall be in the borough of Manhattan. There shall be a branch office in the borough of Brooklyn and a branch office may be established in any of the other boroughs, in the discretion of the board. The salary of the commissioner of buildings for the boroughs of Manhattan and the Bronx, and the salary of the commissioner of buildings for the borough of Brooklyn, shall in each case be $7,000 a year. The salary of the commissioner of buildings for the boroughs of Queens and Richmond shall be $3,500 a year.

Rules and regulations.—Sec. 645. The board shall have the power, by a vote of a majority of its members, to establish general rules and regulations for the administration of the department, and such other rules and regulations as were authorized by law at the time of the passage of this act to be established by the superintendent of buildings in the city of New York, or by the commissioner of the department of buildings in the city of Brooklyn, as said cities were formerly constituted. Such rules and regulations shall, so far as practicable, be uniform in all the boroughs, but the board shall have power, from time to time, to amend or repeal such rules and regulations when in the opinion of a majority of the commissioners it shall seem necessary or desirable. The board shall also have power to appoint a secretary, and within the limits of its appropriation to appoint such subordinate officers as may be necessary for the proper conduct of the office of the department.

General powers of commissioners under existing laws.—Sec. 646. The commissioner for the boroughs of Manhattan and the Bronx shall within such boroughs in addition to the powers, rights and duties expressly conferred or imposed upon him by this act possess and exercise all the powers, rights and duties and shall be subject to all the obligations heretofore vested in, conferred upon or required of the department of buildings or the superintendent of buildings in the city of New York as heretofore constituted, except in so far as the same are inconsistent with or are modified by this act. The commissioner for the borough of Brooklyn shall within such borough in addition to the powers, rights and duties expressly conferred or imposed upon him by this act possess and exercise all the powers, rights and duties, and shall be subject to all the obligations heretofore vested in, conferred upon or required of the department of buildings or the commissioner of the department of buildings in the city of Brooklyn as heretofore constituted, except in so far as the same are inconsistent with or are modified by this act. The commissioner for the boroughs of Queens and Richmond shall within such boroughs respectively in addition to the powers, rights and duties expressly conferred or imposed upon him by this act possess and exercise all the powers, rights and duties and shall be subject to all the obligations heretofore vested in, conferred upon or required of any department, commission, board or officer of Long Island City as heretofore constituted, or of any town or village as heretofore constituted which is comprised within that portion of the county of Queens included in The City of New York as constituted by this act, or which is vested in, conferred upon or required of any department, commission, board or officer of any town or village in the county of Richmond as heretofore constituted, so far as such powers, rights, duties and obligations concern, affect or relate to the construction, alteration or removal of any building or structure erected or to be erected within said boroughs or either of them, except in so far as the same are inconsistent with or are modified by this act.

Continuation and repeal of existing laws ; building code.—Sec. 647. The several acts in effect at the time of the passage of this act concerning, affecting or relating to the construction, alteration or removal of buildings or other structures in any of the municipal and public corporations included within The City of New York, as constituted by this act, are hereby continued in full force and effect in such municipal and public corporations respectively, except in so far as the same are inconsistent with or are modified by this act, provided, however, that the municipal assembly shall have power to establish, and from time to time to amend a code of ordinances, to be known as the Building Code, providing for all matters concerning, affecting or relating to the construction, alteration, or removal of buildings or structures erected or to be erected in The City of New York, as constituted by this act, and for the purpose of preparing such code to appoint and employ a commission of experts; and provided further that upon the establishment of such code the several acts first above mentioned shall cease to have any force or effect, and are hereby repealed, but such repeal shall not take effect until such building code shall be established by the municipal assembly as herein provided.

The provisions of such building code shall be in conformity with and be subject to all general laws of the state concerning, affecting or relating to buildings or classes of buildings, or other structures.

Duties of commissioners; appointment and removal of subordinates.—Sec. 648. Each commissioner shall, within the borough or boroughs in which he is appointed to exercise administrative jurisdiction, have charge of the administration of, and it shall be his duty, subject to and in accordance with the general rules and regulations established by the board, to enforce such rules and regulations and the provisions of this chapter and of such ordinances as may be established by the municipal assembly and of the laws relating to the construction, alteration or removal of buildings or other structures erected or to be erected within such borough or boroughs. Each commissioner within the limits of his appropriation shall have power to appoint and at pleasure to remove subordinate officers, as follows: Such superintendents of buildings, and such inspectors of buildings, engineers, clerks, messengers, assistants and other subordinates as in his judgment may be necessary and proper to carry out and enforce such rules

and regulations and ordinances and the provisions of said
laws and of this chapter within the borough or boroughs
under his jurisdiction. The superintendents of buildings
shall each be a competent architect, engineer or builder of
at least ten years' practice. The inspectors shall be competent men, either architects, engineers, masons, carpen-
ters, plumbers, or iron workers, who shall have served at
least five years as such. It shall not be lawful for any officer or employe in the department to be engaged in conducting or carrying on business as an architect, civil engineer, carpenter, plumber, iron worker, mason or builder
while holding office in the department. Each commissioner
shall have power to designate in writing one of the superintendents of buildings or any of the inspectors so appointed
by him to act on any survey authorized by law, or to perform such other duties as the said commissioners may
direct. Each commissioner may designate a superintendent
of buildings, who, during the absence or inability of any
such commissioner shall possess all the powers and perform all the duties of such commissioner. Any employe,
for any neglect of duty, or omission to properly perform
his duty, or violation of rules, or neglect or disobedience of
orders, or incapacity, or absence without leave, may be
punished by the commissioner appointing him by forfeiting
and withholding pay for a specified time, or by suspension
from duty with or without pay, but this provision shall not
be deemed to abridge the right of said commissioner to
remove or dismiss any inspector of buildings or other subordinate appointed by him or by any predecessor in office
from the service of the department at any time in his discretion.

Decisions of commissioners; appeals.—Sec. 649. Each
commissioner shall have power and it shall be his duty,

subject to the provisions of law and the ordinances of the municipal assembly and the general rules and regulations established by the board, to pass upon any question relative to the mode, manner of construction or materials to be used in the erection or alteration of any building or other structure erected or to be erected within the borough or boroughs under his jurisdiction which is included within the provisions of this chapter or of any existing law applicable to such borough or boroughs relating to the construction, alteration or removal of buildings or other structures, and to require that such mode, manner of construction, or materials shall conform to the true intent and meaning of the several provisions of this chapter and of the laws and ordinances aforesaid and the rules and regulations established by the board. Whenever a commissioner to whom such question has been submitted shall reject or refuse to approve the mode, manner of construction or materials proposed to be followed or used in the erection or alteration of any such building or structure, or when it is claimed that the rules and regulations of the board or the provisions of law or of said ordinances do not apply or that an equally good and more desirable form of construction can be employed in any specific case, the owner of such building or structure, or his duly authorized agent, may appeal from the decision of such commissioner to the board in any case where the amount involved by such decision shall exceed the sum of one thousand dollars; provided, however, that in the boroughs of Manhattan and The Bronx such appeal shall be taken to the board of examiners, established by chapter four hundred and fifty-six of the laws of eighteen hundred and eighty-five and the several acts amendatory thereof or supplemental thereto. The commissioner for the boroughs of Manhattan and The

Bronx shall be ex-officio a member and the chairman of said board of examiners. The other members of said board of examiners shall be the persons mentioned and described in section thirty-one of said chapter four hundred and fifty-six of the laws of eighteen hundred and eighty-five. The appeal authorized by this section may be taken within ten days from the entry of a decision upon the records of the commissioner by filing with the commissioner rendering such decision and with the secretary of the board established by this act or with the clerk of the board of examiners, as the case may be, a notice of appeal stating specifically the questions which the appellant desires to have passed upon by the board of buildings or by the board of examiners, as the case may be, and by filing with the secretary of the board of buildings or the clerk of the board of examiners, as the case may be, copies of all papers required by law or by the rules and regulations of the board of buildings to be submitted to the commissioner upon an application for a building permit, and the board of buildings or the board of examiners, as the case may be, shall thereafter fix a day within a reasonable time for the hearing of such appeal, and upon such hearing the appellant may be represented either in person or by his agent or attorney. The decision of the board of buildings or the board of examiners, as the case may be, upon such appeal, shall be rendered without unnecessary delay and such decision shall be final.

Power to vary the provisions of law.—Sec. 650. Each commissioner shall have power, with the approval of the board, to vary or modify any rule or regulation of the board or the provisions of this chapter or of any existing law or ordinance relating to the construction, alteration or removal of any building or structure erected or to be erected within his jurisdiction upon an application to him therefor in writing by the owner of such building or structure or his duly authorized agent, where there are practical difficulties in the way of carrying out the strict letter of the law, so that the spirit of the law shall be observed and public safety secured and substantial justice done ; but no such variation or modification shall be granted or allowed except by a vote of a majority of the board. Where such application has been filed with a commissioner the owner of such building or structure or his duly authorized agent shall have the right to present a petition to such commissioner and the board, setting forth the grounds for the desired variation or modification, and may appear before said board and be heard. The board shall fix a date within a reasonable time for a hearing upon such application and shall as soon as practicable render a decision thereon, which decision shall be final. The particulars of each such application and of the decision of the board thereon shall be entered upon the records of the board, and if the application is granted a certificate therefor shall be issued by the commissioner to whom the application is made and shall be countersigned by the secretary of the board.

Accounts ; annual estimates ; expenditures.—Sec. 651. Each commissioner shall keep accurate and detailed accounts, in a form to be approved by the commissioners of accounts, of all moneys received and expended by him, the sources from which they are received and the purposes for which they are expended, and shall prepare itemized monthly statements of all receipts and expenditures in duplicate, one of which statements, together with all vouchers, shall be filed with the controller, and one of which shall be filed in his own office. Each commissioner shall, on or about the first day of September in each year prepare an itemized estimate of his necessary expenses for the ensuing fiscal year and present the same to the board. The three estimates so prepared as revised by the board shall together constitute the annual estimate of the department of buildings, and shall be submitted to the board of estimate and apportionment within the time prescribed by this act for the submission of estimates for the several departments of the city. No commissioner shall incur any expense for any purpose in excess of the amount appropriated therefor ; nor shall he expend any money so appropriated for any purpose other than that for which it was appropriated.

Record of applications.—Sec. 652. Each commissioner shall keep a record of all applications presented to him concerning, affecting or relating to the construction, alteration or removal of buildings or other structures. Such record shall include the date of the filing of each such application ; the name and address of the applicant ; the name and address of the owner of the land on which the structure mentioned in such application is situated ; the names and addresses of the architect and builder employed thereon ; a designation of the premises by street number, or otherwise sufficient to identify the same ; a statement of the nature and proposed use of such structure ; and a brief statement of the nature of the application, together with a memorandum of the decision of the commissioner upon such application and the date of the rendition of such decision. The books containing such records are hereby declared to be public records, and shall be open to inspection at all reasonable times.

Fire Department.—The head of the Fire Department is the Fire Commissioner. There are over 2,000 paid firemen.

Volunteer Firemen retained.—The members of existing volunteer fire departments in the former suburban villages and towns are to be preferred, so far as practicable, for appointment in the paid department. (Sec. 722.)

Fire Hydrants are to be kept clear from Snow and ice in the street for ten feet each side of the hydrant from the curb to the centre of the street *by the owner or lessee of the adjoining* premises; $10 fine if you don't do it, besides paying the expense of clearing it. (Sec. 750.)

Pulling down buildings to prevent spread of fire.— The Fire Commissioner has power to do this whenever he judges it necessary. If it should occur, then the value of the building is afterwards to be ascertained by a jury, and paid to the owner in the manner provided for taking land for public purposes. (Sec. 754.)

Chimney afire.—No matter what the cause, if any chimney, stove-pipe or flue takes fire the *occupant of the premises* must pay $5 fine. (Sec. 760.)

Hoistways, iron-shutters, well-holes and trap-doors must be closed at the completion of business each day : $50 fine for every neglect or omission of each *occupant* to do so ; and for any accident or injury to life or limb resulting from such neglect or omission, the person culpable or negligent shall be liable *not less than* $1,000 to the person injured, and in case of death *not less than* $5,000 to his family or relatives. (Sec. 761.)

Places of Amusement, theatres, and other public buildings, are to be protected from fire as directed in Sec. 762.

Gunpowder and other Explosives can only be sold, or kept, in small quantities, and under license from the Fire Commissioners, as prescribed by section 763.

Fireworks and Petroleum, etc., also, as prescribed by sections 764 to 768.

Chemicals and cotton, hay and other vegetable products very combustible, are governed by Secs. 769, 780.

Right to Enter Buildings.—The Fire Commissioner and his officers and agents have the right to enter your house and store and any building to examine whether any combustibles are stored there, and, if there has been a fire, to investigate its origin.   (Secs. 771, 780.)

These sections of the new charter, relating to fires and their extinction, sections 748 to 783, doubtless supersede the sections of the former Consolidation Act (chapter 410, sections 446 to 468, Laws of 1882,) relating to the same subject.

Docks, Piers, Harbor, Port and Waters.—(Secs. 816 to 881.)

Department of Docks and Ferries.—The head of this Department is the *Board of Docks*, three Commissioners.

Repairing, building, leasing, cleaning, dredging all wharves, piers, slips, docks, etc., are in the exclusive charge of the Board of Docks.   (Sec. 818.)

Lands under Water Owned by the State must be conveyed to The City of New York by the State Commissioners of the Land Office whenever the Board of Docks may deem it necessary for the construction of wharves, docks, slips, etc. (Sec. 831.)

" Property " and " Wharf Property," whenever used in chapter XVI. of the new charter (the one relating to Docks and Waters), shall be taken to mean not only all wharves, piers, docks, bulkheads, slips and basins, but the land beneath the same, and all rights, privileges and easements appurtenant thereto, and such upland or made land adjacent to said wharves, etc., jurisdiction over which upland and made land may be assigned to the Department of Docks and Ferries by the Commissioners of the Sinking Fund. (Sec. 833.)

Floating Baths.—The Board of Docks must furnish sites for these free of charge, where designated by the Commissioner of Public Buildings. (Sec. 834.)

Public Markets and Wharves may be erected and kept by The City of New York over the waters of the East and North Rivers, adjoining any of its docks or wharves. (Sec. 835.)

Recreation Piers, Fire Department Piers and Docks for the Street Cleaning Department may be designated and set apart by the Board of Docks under sections 836 to 838.

Sheds on Piers or Bulkheads must be regulated, in their construction, by the Board of Docks. (Sec. 844.)

Canal Boats, exclusively, are to have the East River from the west side of pier No. 3 to and including the east side of pier No. 8, and no other vessels can go in that section of waterfront between March 20th and December 31st of each year.   (Sec. 854.)

Docks set apart for Garden Produce are on the Hudson River from Gansevoort St. to Little West 12th St. (Sec. 858.)

Wharfage and Dockage Rates will be found enumerated in section 859 of the charter ; also in Secs. 860 to 863.

What Waters included in the Port of New York.—These are all the waters of the North and East Rivers and the harbor embraced within or adjacent to or opposite to the shores of The City of New York.   (Sec. 864.)

Grants of Land under Water Restricted.—No such grants shall be made by the Municipal Assembly, or by any officer or board, beyond the exterior lines of the City of New York, as fixed by Act of the Legislature, April 17th, 1857, as amended.   (Sec. 876.)

Time for Improving Lands Adjacent to Water on Harlem River.—The period of time fixed for the appropriation to the purposes of commerce by the construction of a dock or docks, and filling in the same, in all letters patent, issued by the People of the State of New York to the owners of the adjacent upland for lands under water, and, between high and low water mark in front of and adjacent to the lands of the said owners of the adjacent upland on the easterly shore of the Harlem River, is extended until two years after the time when plans for the improvement of said river shall have been or shall be completed by the proper authorities, and copies of such plans filed, one in the New York Register's Office and one in the Office of the Secretary of State at Albany. (Sec. 877.)

Department of Taxes and Assessments.—The head of this department is called the *Board of Taxes and Assessments*, composed of five commissioners, one of whom is appointed as President of the Board, and one of whom must be a learned lawyer. (Sec. 885.)

Taxes and Assessments are governed by sections 876 to 964; assessments more especially by the last twenty-three sections. (Sec. 942 to 964.)

Correction of Assessed Valuation may be applied for under section 895 during the time that the books are open to public inspection, from the second Monday of January to the first day of May every year (except 1898, when they will be open from the first Monday of February to the first day of May). Application for correction of the assessed value of *real estate* must be made in writing, stating the ground of objection. Then the Board will act on it. (Sec. 895.)

Applications in each borough may be made to a deputy tax commissioner appointed for that Borough by the Board, and he can take testimony upon the matter, and transmit it, with his opinion, to the Board. (Sec. 898.)

Taxes for 1898 in Brooklyn, Queens and Richmond will be levied in 1897.

Taxes for old New York City for 1897 have been levied in 1897.

To Prevent Double Taxation there shall be no taxes levied in 1898, in Brooklyn, Queens and Richmond.

The 1897 taxes levied in the latter part of that year in Brooklyn, Queens and Richmond will go into the receipts of the new City for the purposes and disbursements of 1898, and if it transpires that the amount received from any Borough from these 1897 taxes is either more or less than its due proportion of the expenses of the new city, such excess or deficit shall be equalized in the budget of the year 1899 ; and the Municipal Assembly can lay different rates of taxation in the several Boroughs, in 1899, so as to bring about this proper proportion. (Sec. 901.)

Different rates in each Borough each year will be necessary in order to pay the salaries of the *county* officers, and the other *county* charges and exp.nses in the *Counties* of New York, Kings and Richmond (all of which counties are entirely within the new city), and the proportion that will be due to Queens County from that part of Queens County included in The City of New York. (Sec. 902.)

In forming the new City the Legislature did not abolish nor change the existing *county* organizations.

Permits for Buildings must be filed, by copy, within five days, with the Department of Taxes and Assessments, by the officer who issues the permit. (Sec. 903.)

Exempt from taxation, every building for public worship, and every schoolhouse or other seminary of learning, within the city, only when *exclusively* used for such purpose, and exclusively the property of a religious society. (Sec. 904.)

Decisions of the Board of Taxes and Assessments can be reviewed by certiorari to the Supreme Court. (Sec. 906.)

Majority Clause.—A determination or decision required or authorized by this charter, when made by a majority of any body or board, shall be held to be the determination or decision of the body or board. (Sec. 908.)

Taxes are Due and Payable at the offices in the several boroughs where the property is. (Sec. 913.)

Rebates for prompt payment and *penalties* for delay remain as at present in old New York.

Undivided Parts of Taxes, where a sum of money in gross has been taxed upon any land, may be paid by any person claiming any divided or undivided part of the premises, and the remainder may be sold if the balance of the tax remains unpaid. (Sec. 920.)

Distress and Sale for Personal Taxes remaining unpaid may be ordered by the Receiver of Taxes, and the marshal can levy on and sell not only the goods and chattels of the person against whom the warrant is issued, but *any* goods and chattels in his or her possession, *no matter whom they may belong to.* (Sec. 926.) The assessed valuation for personal taxes is over $400,000,000.

Unpaid Taxes and Assessments prior to January 1st, 1898, from Kings, Queens and Richmond counties, shall be due and payable thereafter to The City of New York, and all tax and assessment lists in the hands of any officer of any of the places within the new city limits must be turned over to the Comptroller on that day, January 1st, 1898.

Assessments for Local Improvements are to be made by a *Board of Assessors*, not by the Commissioners of Taxes and Assessments ; but this is only in cases other than those required by law to be confirmed by a court of record. (Sec. 943.)

A **Board of Revision of Assessments,** composed of the Comptroller, Corporation Counsel and President of the Board of Public Improvements, has the powers and duties of revision, correction and confirmation of local assessments, other than those confirmed by the Board of Assessors or by a court, and may consider on the merits all objections made to any such assessment, and may subpœna and examine witnesses, and may confirm the assessment or refer it back to the Board of Assessors for revisal and correction.   If not referred back within thirty days, such assessments shall be deemed to be confirmed.   (Sec. 944.)

Not more than half the fair value of any house or lot, improved or unimproved land, can be assessed in any case.   (Sec. 947.)   It is a comfort to know this.

No assessment for repairing can be laid *inside the limits of the old city*. But in Brooklyn, Queens and Richmond you *can* be assessed for repairing.   (Sec. 948.)

Notice of Completion of Assessments is to be given in the "City Record."   (Sec. 950.)   The labor of following these up and finding them out, in that excellent but multifarious sheet, will be saved by those who are subscribers to the **Real Estate Record and Guide,** which will continue to publish all such information in regard to real estate, as it has done for years past.

No liability to owners for originally establishing a grade after January 1st, 1898, but only for a *change* of established grade where an owner has built in accordance with it; and you must make your claim for this at the time and place for which notice is given by the Board of Assessors in the "City Record." (Secs. 951, 952, 953.)

Assessments for Deepening Water in Docks, etc., may be laid on adjoining owners. (Sec. 954.)

No suit can be brought to vacate an assessment for local improvements other than those confirmed by a court of record, but any party aggrieved is confined to the course marked out in Secs. 958 to 953, whether the objection be for fraud or any substantial error.

Re-assessment.—And any lands which may be discharged from an assessment for fraud or irregularity in it may have a new corrected assessment laid and collected for the improvement. (Sec. 964.)

Opening Streets and Parks is to be done in the old way, by application to the Supreme Court, and appointment of commissioners of estimate and assessment. I do not give the details of these proceedings, laid down in Sec. 970 to 1011, because every sensible man will in such matters

Get a lawyer, either your own regular counsel, or if you have none, employ one familiar with the new charter and with such proceedings.

No streets can be opened in the grounds of St. John's College, Fordham ; nor those of the University of The City of New York ; nor those of Columbia College. (Sec. 972.)

The City is to own the land at once upon the report being filed, if the land is vacant, *or six months* from the day the report is filed, *if there are buildings upon it*, in every case, *where the Board of Public Improvements deem it for the public interest*, and may immediately take possession, and in such cases interest is to run in favor of the owners, from the date title vests in the City. In all other cases title shall vest in the City upon the confirmation of the Commissioners' report by the Court. (Sec. 990.)

Owners may convey to the City, without any condemnation proceedings; if their title is clear, and, if they give a deed, with an abstract of title and complete searches, and pay for recording the deed ; and the lots fronting on such parcels shall not be chargeable with any portion of the expense of opening any of the rest of that street, except a fair proportion of the awards made for damages for buildings. (Sec. 992.) This may be of value in the outlying portions of the new City.

The City may agree with owners of some or all parcels about the cost and damages and benefits of any such a street opening, or other improvement, and after such an agreement duly executed it shall be as binding as an assessment regularly made. (Sec. 994.) Obviously a great deal of the expense may thus sometimes be saved.

Contracts between Landlords and Tenants regarding land taken by the City *cease*, determine, and become absolutely discharged upon the vesting of the title in the City, where the *whole* of the lot or parcel is taken, and shall similarly cease *as to the part taken*, where only a part *is* taken. (Sec. 996.)

Notice of Confirmation of Assessment is to be published by the comptroller in the "City Record." (Sec. 1005.)

Interest at seven per cent. is to be charged on all assessments not paid within sixty days, sections 1006, 1019 ; and on all arrears of taxes. (Sec. 1020.)

Water Rents in same bill with Taxes after this. (Sec. 1024.)

On June First Taxes and Water Rates become arrears. (Sec. 1023.) And have to pay seven per cent. per annum interest from date of confirmation.

Sales for unpaid Taxes and Assessments are to be made *three* years after confirmation. (Sec. 1027.)

Sales for unpaid Water Rents are to be made *four* years after they were due. (Sec. 1027.)

I do not find that any date is fixed in the charter for the payment of Water Rates ; but unless they are paid by August 1st, five per cent penalty attaches, and unless paid by November 1st, 10 per cent. (Sec. 476) ; and as the Commissioner of Water Supply is to turn over all unpaid water rents to the Collector of Arrears, at the time the tax levy is confirmed each year, section 1022, (which is on or about September 1st), it is best to assume that the old date, May 1st, remains the first date upon which water rents can annually be paid.

Lands heretofore sold and bid in for taxes or assessments by any village, town or city now consolidated shall belong to the new city. (Sec. 1033.)

Mortgagees are to be notified of sale before the time to redeem expires. (Secs. 1036 to 1040.)

Notice of Expiration of Time to Redeem is to be published twice a week for six weeks in the City Record (Sec. 1041.)

Additional Details of Sale for Taxes, and of Redemption are to be found in sections 1042 to 1054, as well as in sections 1017 to 1042.

The title to all real estate purchased for school purposes (except the State Normal School at Jamaica), is vested in The City of New York. But all suits in relation to such property must be brought in the name of the Board of Education. (Sec. 1055.)

Taxes for School purposes are to be raised in *two* funds, "The special school fund" and "The general school fund."

New school-houses, and sites, with repairs, etc., are to be raised in the *special* school fund, and the Board of Estimate and Apportionment must indicate in the budget the respective amounts of this special fund which shall be available for each of the four school boards (Manhattan and The Bronx, Brooklyn, Queens, and Richmond). (Sec. 1060.)

A **Superintendent of School Buildings** is to be appointed by the Board of Education, and he may appoint four deputy superintendents; one for each Borough. All plans for new school buildings, and for alterations, must be approved by the Superintendent. (Sec. 1074.)

Board of Health.—The head of the Department of Health is the Board of Health, consisting of the President of the Board of Police, the Health Officer of the Port, and three Commissioners of Health appointed by the Mayor. (Sec. 1167.)

The Board of Health has power to take possession of, and occupy for temporary hospitals, *any* building or buildings in the City, during the prevalence of an epidemic.

And shall pay a just compensation for private property so taken. (Sec. 1170.)

Repairs of Buildings.—The Board of Health has power to order and enforce the repairs of buildings, houses, and other structures; the regulation and control of all public markets (so far as relates to the cleanliness, ventilation and drainage, and to the prevention of the sale of improper articles); the removal of any obstruction, matter or thing in or upon the public streets, sidewalks or places, dangerous to life or health; the prevention of accidents endangering life or health; and generally the abating of all nuisances. (Sec. 1171.)

The Sanitary Code, (Sec. 1172), contains about 225 sections in itself. And you are bound by them all, and liable to the penalties for their breach, whether you know what is in them or not. At least forty of these sections bear directly or indirectly upon the ownership of real estate in this City, and, in the language of section 205 of that code (edition of 1896), " The *owner*, lessee, tenant or occupant of *any* building or premises, or of any part thereof, where there shall be * * * *a violation of any* ordinance or *section of* the Sanitary Code, *shall be* jointly and severally *liable* therefor." So the best thing you can do is to obtain from the Health Department a copy of the Sanitary Code. It governs all parts of the new City, and privies in the suburbs of Jamaica or of Hempstead must hereafter be built in accordance with sections 119, 192 and 206 of this Code, and the owners of cows on Staten Island must hasten to get permits to keep them within the City limits, in accordance with section 200, or each will be guilty of a misdemeanor and liable to fine and imprisonment. Does your tenant, who keeps a boarding house, allow too many people to sleep in one room ? Do you know ? You are liable, whether you know or not.

Alteration of old buildings, erection of new buildings must conform to this Sanitary Code as well as to the Building laws. Sidewalks must be kept clear of water and ice, and from other obstructions ; manufactories must burn their own smoke ; receptacles must be provided for ashes and for garbage for the Street Cleaning Department ; contagious diseases must be reported ; hatchways and well-holes must be inclosed ; waste or soil pipes of tenements and lodging houses must be ventilated ; sunken lots kept clean and fenced ; and a score of other details be attended to in accordance with this Sanitary Code, or the expense of having them done by the Health Department becomes a lien upon your real estate (like an assessment), and you, the owner, although absent traveling, and ignorant of your tenant's neglect and breach of the code, become liable to fine and imprisonment. (Secs. 1172, 1278 and 1222 of Charter.) So send and get a copy of that Code.

Dangerous Buildings, and Places.—Whenever any building, erection, excavation, premises, business pursuit, matter or thing, or the sewerage, drainage or ventilation thereof, shall be in a condition or in effect dangerous to life or health, the Board of Health may take sufficient proof to authorize declaring it a public nuisance, or dangerous to life or health, and may order it to be removed, or altered or improved.

Stay or modification of such an order may be applied for within three days after service, or *attempted* service, by the party served, or *intended to be served.*

This is an outrageous power. So long as the Board *intended* to serve the owner, or *attempted* to do so, unless he applies for a hearing within three days from the attempt to serve him, his rights may be taken away, and possibly great damage done to him, often by mistake, and without his having even heard of the matter. It *may* be that this power will never be wrongfully used.   But no such power ought ever to be granted.

The situation is not bettered by the additional power that if the order (which he may never have heard of) is not complied with within five days, the Board of Health can have it done, and all the expenses are to be a charge against each of the owners or part owners of the building, and each of the lessees and occupants, and a lien on all rent due, or to grow due, for the use of any place, room, building or premises ; and the Board of Health *can assign the bill*, and its assignee can sue on and recover it.   (Sec. 1176.)

I say this is an outrageous law to impose upon citizens in a free country.   And no man surpasses me in allegiance to the laws, or in a desire to conform to and to uphold a rigid enforcement of all sanitary rules for the benefit of the community, and especially for the benefit of the poor, or those whose means and industry do not leave them time to protect themselves.   But no such unfair powers ought ever to be intrusted to any man or Board.

Delegation of Powers.—The Board of Health may from time to time delegate *any portion of its powers* to the Sanitary Superintendent, or to an Assistant Sanitary Superintendent.   (Sec. 1182.)

Examinations and Surveys.—The members of the Board of Health, the Health Commissioners, the Sanitary Superintendent, the Assistant Sanitary Superintendent, and any of the Sanitary Inspectors, and such other officer or person as may, at any time, be authorized by the Board of Health, may enter, examine and survey all grounds, erections, structures, apartments, buildings, and every part thereof, all cellars, sewers, passages and excavations, and inspect the sanitary condition thereof. (Sec. 1188.)

Duties of Owners, Lessees, and Occupants, in any place, room, stall, apartment, and building, to keep and preserve the same and every part of it, and the sewerage, drainage, and ventilation in such condition that it shall not be a nuisance, nor dangerous, nor prejudicial to health. (Sec. 1201.)

Offensive Trades can not be lawfully carried on within the Borough of *Manhattan*. It is all right to do so in the other Boroughs. These trades are enumerated in Sec. 1212 as bone boiling, bone burning, bone grinding, horse skinning, cow skinning, or skinning of dead animals, or the boiling of offal, but *not* the slaughtering or dressing of animals for sale in said City.

Filling in Lands.—This cannot be done anywhere in the new City with garbage, dead animals, decaying matter, or any offensive and unwholesome material, or with dirt or ashes mixed with any such thing. (Sec. 1213.)

Yards and Cellars.—The Board of Health can pass ordinances for the filling, draining and regulating of any grounds, yards or cellars, and also sunken lots extending into the rivers or Long Island Sound ; and for filling, altering and amending all sinks and privies, and for causing subterraneous drains to be made from the latter. (Sec. 1214.)

Right of Way.—The Board of Health can acquire *rights of way* over, under or through lands, for *drains* other than sewers. (Sec. 1216.)

The proceedings for acquiring such rights of way are similar to those for acquiring the absolute ownership of land for streets, but the details are laid down in sections 1217, 1218.

Punishment for Violating any Order of the Board of Health is a fine not exceeding $250, or imprisonment not exceeding six months, or both ; it being a misdemeanor.

Violation of any part of the Sanitary Code is also a misdemeanor, and also a fine of $50.

Separate Receptacles for Ashes and Garbage shall be required by the Board of Health, also for rubbish. And they can only be put out on sidewalks at the times designated by the Commissioner of Street Cleaning, and for any violations of these provisions of the sanitary code *both the owners and* the occupants of *all* houses in the city shall be separately responsible and subject to the penalties and prosecutions imposed by said code, and all other provisions of the city ordinances relative to the cleanliness of the streets. (Sec. 1223.)

Which is another outrageous law.

Service of Orders.—Quite in keeping with these unfair provisions of this law is the fact that, under section 1224, you can be sent to jail and fined for breach of an order, quite likely unjust, and granted, or entered as a matter of course by some employe of the Board, without due hearing, and which order has been served on some one you employed to collect your rents, and who has forgotten to report it to you ; no matter, *that* service is enough to bind you and everybody, as if made upon the owners, lessees, tenants, and occupants of the building.

Public health ought to be preserved and cared for most thoroughly, but not at such a cost of private rights and liberties, without due process of law.   The fact that such a statute has been passed, does not make it " due process of law."

A nuisance under this statute embraces not only what is known as a public nuisance at common law, or in equity jurisprudence, but also whatever is dangerous to human life or detrimental to health ; whatever building or erection, or part or cellar thereof, is overcrowded with occupants, or is not provided with adequate ingress and egress to and from the same, or the apartments thereof, or is not sufficiently supported, ventilated, sewered, drained, cleaned or lighted, in reference to their or its intended or actual use ; and whatever renders the air, or human food or drink, unwholesome, are also, severally, in contemplation of this act, nuisances ; and all such nuisances are declared illegal. (Sec. 1229.)   As they ought to be.

Overcrowding in Cars and Elevators.—But all this will not prevent people being allowed to be jammed and packed

5

together in elevated railroads and surface cars, and in elevators, like so many sardines, only not so clean ; dumb, driven cattle, buttock to face, male and female, in the most disgusting manner, detrimental to health, comfort and morals, a nuisance under that section 1229.   This, however, is because there are so few *real* Americans in New York City, people with respect for themselves and consideration for others.   You would expect it to be different. But to see that it is not you have only to look daily at what the citizens of New York both endure themselves and force upon others in this regard.   The remedy is to fine every conductor who carries more than he has seats for, and every person who insists upon forcing himself in where there are no seats.   Straps to hang upon ought to be abolished.   Ostensibly they were forced on the railroad companies for the "safety" of passengers.   What a trick of those companies to make it lawful to carry additional passengers standing upon the feet of those sitting !   And every person, man or woman, who *attempts* to stand in between the seats of *open* cars ought forthwith to be arrested and fined "ten dollars or ten days."   If the various railroads and traction companies do not or can not furnish enough vehicles, take away their charters, or grant more charters to more companies.

But whether it is because four out of five of all its citizens were so unfortunate as to be born abroad in monarchical countries, (they or their immediate parents,) or whatever the cause, the disappointing fact remains that the demo-

•ratic, republican, citizens of this great city, are wanting in self respect and in respect for the rights of others.

Boarding and Lodging House Keepers shall, whenever required by the Department of Health, report in writing the name of each person sick in their houses, within twelve hours after each case of sickness occurs. (Sec. 1250.)

Every Owner, and Part Owner, and Person Interested, Lessee, Tenant and Occupant of, or in, any place, water, ground, room, stall, apartment, building, erection, vessel, vehicle, matter and thing in The City of New York, and every person conducting or interested in business, is bound to keep, place and preserve every building, plot of ground, etc., subject to the ordinances of the Sanitary Code and the orders of the Board of Health, and is both jointly and separately liable personally for all the expenses the Board of Health choose to incur in carrying out any order of that Board. These expenses are also a lien on any and all rent due to a landlord ; and the Board of Health can assign each claim for any such expenses, and the assignee can sue for them. (Secs. 1275, 1276, 1277.)

All the proceedings of the Health Department are presumed to be just and legal. (Sec. 1261.)

Expenses of Board of Health shall be a lien on the property, filed like a mechanic's lien, and ahead of all mortgages and other liens, except taxes and assessments. (Sec. 1278.)

Your tenant must pay a judgment against you and

deduct it from his rent where it was obtained by the Board of Health.   (Sec. 1279, subdivision 4.)

As stated before (page 62), all this can happen, under this despotic law, without your ever having heard of the matter or knowing anything about it.

A **judgment declaring a nuisance to exist,** and ordering it abated or remedied, and for costs and expenses and penalties therefor, is a lien on the real property to which the nuisance related.   (Sec. 1290.)

An injunction may be granted in any suit brought by the Health Department to abate a nuisance, and in the injunction order the court may require any building, erection or grounds to be put in condition that will not be dangerous to life or health, before the same shall be leased, rented or occupied, or before any rent shall be collected for the use of the whole or any portion of the same; and the court can, in any such injunction order, require any and all tenants, lessees, and occupants to pay their rent to the Health Department, and the latter to pay it out on account of expenses of putting the premises in good sanitary condition.   (Sec. 1297.)

Tenement and Lodging Houses must conform in construction, appurtenances, and premises to the requirements of the charter.   (Secs. 1304 to 1325.)

This tenement-house law goes into a great variety of details which need not be fully repeated here, because any one intending to build, or buy, will naturally read these sections in the charter itself.

No property owner in The City of New York can hereafter get along safely without a copy of the charter itself ; or what is better, a copy of Van Siclen's

"**Analytical Index to the Charter** of The City of New York," now going to press (December, 1897) ; this form of Index contains *every* item of *all* the statute, briefly and clearly stated.

The Sanitary Code of course applies to tenement houses.

Halls.—If such a house is occupied by more than one family on a floor, and if the halls do not open directly on the external air, with suitable windows, without a room or other obstruction at the end, it cannot be used nor rented unless sufficient light and ventilation are provided for to the satisfaction of the Department of Buildings and the Department of Health.   (Sec. 1302.)

A **tenement-house is** any house or building, or portion thereof, which is let to be occupied as the home or residence of three families or more, living independently of each other, and doing their cooking upon the premises ; or by more than two families upon any floor, so living and cooking, but having a common right in the halls, stairways, yards, water-closets or privies, or some of them. (Sec. 1305.)

A **lodging house is** any house or building, or portion thereof, in which persons are harbored, or received, or lodged, for hire for a single night, or for less than a week at one time, or any part of which is let for any person to sleep in for any term less than a week.   (Sec. 1305.)

A **cellar is** every basement or lower story of any building or house, of which one half or more of the height from floor to the ceiling is below the level of the street adjoining.   (Sec. 1305.)

Roofs must be kept in good repair.

Water from roof carried off ; no dripping.

Stairs must have proper banisters and railings, and be kept in good repair.

A fire escape on every such house.   (Sec. 1306.)

Every sleeping room which does not communicate directly with the external air must have a transom over the door into the next room which communicates with the external air, and another transom over the door into the hall.

A **ventilator** must be in the roof at the top of the hall. (Sec. 1307.)

A **water closet,** ventilated, for every fifteen occupants.

Separate sewer connection for each tenement house, or lodging house.

No privy, or vault or cesspool in, under, or connected with any such house (except by special permit).

Where there is no sewer to connect with, the yard and area must have a covered drain into the street gutter to carry off surface water.   (Sec. 1308.)

Cellars and Basements can not be constructed to be occupied as dwellings, without a permit from the Department of Buildings, nor without conforming to many details in section 1309.

Cellars and Vaults can not be used as sleeping rooms.

Wall paper must be removed every time, and walls and ceiling cleansed, before any new wall paper can be put on.

Every part must be kept clean.

Owner must clean as often as Board of Health orders : so must any lessee of any part.

Whitewash walls and ceilings at least once every year. (Sec. 1310.)

Bakeries ; Transoms, Windows and Doors must be solidly closed up between upper floors of tenement or lodging houses and the hall of the basement or first floor where there is a bakery in which fat is boiled ; and such a tenement must be fireproof, or the ceiling and side walls of the bakery be fireproof.

Paint, Oil, Liquor and Drug stores, all their transoms and windows opening into halls, must be closed solidly, or glazed with wire glass, and all doors be fireproof, where there is a tenement or lodging house above. (Sec. 1311.)

Receptacles for garbage and other refuse must be supplied.

No part can be used to store any combustible article.

No domestic animals can be kept (except dogs and cats). (Sec. 1312.)

Address and name of every owner must be filed by him with the Health Department, with a description of his tenement house or lodging house.

Upon selling a tenement house or lodging house both buyer and seller must file a notice of the transfer with the Health Department.

In case of a Will, the executor, and the devisee of such a house, must both file notice of the new ownership of the latter, within thirty days after probate of the will.

Heirs, where there is no will, must file notice of their having become the owners.

Administrator must file such a notice, if there is no will, and the heirs are under age, and have no guardian, within thirty days after the death of the owner.

Notices to tenement house and lodging house owners are served by *not* serving them, but by posting them up in some conspicuous place in the house, five days before time for doing the thing required. It is the duty of the Health Department to also mail on the same day, a copy of such notice to the address given by the owner ; but that posting of notice in the house is declared by the law sufficient service of the notice on the owner. (Sec. 1313.)

Inspection Twice a Year.

Free access to the house for all health officers.

The owner or keeper of any lodging house, and the owner, agent and lessee of any tenement house or any part of it, shall give notice at once to the Health Department of any case of infectious disease, *if information thereof has been given* to such owner, keeper, agent or lessee. (Sec. 1314.)

This section of the law is remarkable in that it does *not*

punish the owner with fine and imprisonment in case he has not been informed of the misfortune that has befallen him.

Infected and Uninhabitable Houses may be condemned by the Board of Health, and all persons ordered to vacate, until the building has been repaired and made habitable. (Sec. 1315.)

Old or Infected House may be torn down after condemnation by Board of Health, and after due proceedings in court, and in this case fair damages are to be awarded to the owner on the basis laid down in section 1316.

Houses hereafter erected must comply with all the requirements of sections 1318 to 1325, in regard to **space of lot occupied, size of rooms, ventilation, chimneys, ash receptacles, water, cellar floor, ceilings, gas, overcrowding, janitor, penalties for violations, etc.**

Construction of tenement houses and space prescribed for building the same.—Sec. 1,318. It shall not be lawful, without a permit from the department of buildings, to alter, erect or convert to the purposes of a tenement or lodging house, a building on any lot where there is another building on the same lot; nor shall it be lawful to build or to erect any building on any lot whereon there is already a tenement or lodging house, unless there is a clear open space exclusively belonging thereto, and extending upward from the ground, of at least ten feet between said buildings if they are one story high above the level of the ground; if they are two stories high the distance between them shall not be less than fifteen feet; if they are three stories high the distance then shall not be less than twenty feet; if they are more than three stories

high the distance between them shall not be less than
twenty-five feet, but when thorough ventilation of such
open spaces can be otherwise secured, such distances may
be lessened or modified in special cases by a permit from
the department of buildings. At the rear of every building hereafter erected for or converted to the purposes of a
tenement or lodging house on any lot, there shall be and
remain a clear open space of not less than ten feet between
it and the rear end of the lot. No one continuous building hereafter constructed shall be built or converted
to the purposes of a tenement or lodging house in
the city of New York, upon an ordinary city lot, and
no existing tenement or lodging house shall be enlarged
or altered, or its lot be diminished, so that it shall occupy
more than sixty-five per centum of the area of said lot, but
where the light and ventilation of such tenement or lodging house, are, in the opinion of the superintendent of
buildings, materially improved, he may permit such tenement or lodging house to occupy an area not exceeding
seventy-five per centum of the said lot, and in the same
proportion if the lot be greater or less in size than twenty-
five by one hundred feet; but this provision shall not
apply to corner lots, in which, however, no such building
hereafter constructed, above the first story, shall occupy
more than ninety-two per centum of the area of a lot, and
no such building shall come within five feet of the rear of
said lot, provided, further, that in all cases, both for
corner and interior lots, the interior courts or shafts shall
not be less than two feet four inches wide at their narrow-
est parts. In computing the amount of the lot covered by a
building, any shaft or court of less than twenty-five square
feet in area shall be considered as part of the building and
not as part of the free air space. No shaft or court, over

ten square feet in area, hereafter constructed in a tenement house or lodging house, except elevator shafts or staircase wells, shall be covered with a roof, skylight or otherwise. In all tenement houses hereafter constructed, or buildings hereafter converted to the purposes of a tenement house, the stairway communicating between said cellar or basement and the floor next above, when placed within any such building, shall be inclosed with brick walls, and such stairway shall be provided with fire-proof doors at the top and bottom of said flight of stairs. An open area shall be constructed from the level of the cellar to the sidewalk in front and extending the full width of such houses, with a staircase to give access to the cellar from the street. Where stores are located on the first floor the area may be covered with suitable vault lights or gratings. In all tenement houses hereafter constructed, or buildings hereafter converted to the purposes of a tenement house, the openings to the elevators or lifts in the cellar, and at every opening, on every story, shall be provided with self-closing fire-proof doors. This provision, however, shall not apply to such elevators in tenement houses as are operated by a conductor stationed within the car ; but if such elevators run to the cellar, they must be inclosed in the cellar with fire-proof walls, and the door to the cellar, if any, must be fire-proof and self-closing. In all tenement houses hereafter constructed, or buildings hereafter converted to the purposes of a tenement house, all staircases shall be fire-proof; but this provision as to staircases shall not apply to buildings which are not over five stories high above the cellar, and which contain not more than three suites of rooms on a floor. Every tenement house hereafter constructed, or buildings hereafter converted to the purpose of a tenement house, exceeding three stories in height, or having a basement with three stories above the cellar, shall have the entrance hall and entire stairwell and stairs, built of slow-burning construction or fire-proof material; no wainscoting shall be allowed in the main halls except of cement, or other fire-proof material; at least one flight of such stairs shall extend to the roof, and be inclosed in a bulkhead building of fire-proof material. In all tenement houses hereafter constructed, and buildings hereafter converted to the purposes of a tenement house, each room must have a separate window opening into the outer air; each water-closet must have a window opening into the outer air, and such water-closet inclosure, if provided with a ventilating flue or duct, may have the window opening on any court or shaft containing at least twenty-five square feet in area; the floor of each water-closet must be made water-proof with asphalt, cement, tile, metal or some other water-proof material; and such water-proofing must extend at least sixteen inches above the floor, except at the door opening so that said floor can be washed or flushed out without leaking. The light and ventilation of all buildings hereafter erected for, or converted to the purpose of tenement or lodging houses, must be provided in accordance with the requirements of this title, and the conditions of a plan and permit previously approved in writing by the department of buildings, and no existing tenement or lodging house shall be enlarged or altered, or its lot diminished without a similar permit. The department of buildings is hereby empowered, and directed to make rules and regulations not inconsistent with the requirements of this title, and which in addition to the requirements of this title, shall be the conditions of approval of the plans and permits; these rules and regulations shall govern the arrangement and distribution of the uncovered area, size, lighting, location and arrangement of shafts, rooms, cellars, and halls. No building or premises occupied for a tenement house shall be used for a lodging house, private school, stable, or for the storage and handling of rags, but the department of health may, by a special permit, fixing the conditions thereof in writing, and providing there be the necessary cubic air space and ventilation, allow the maintenance of a private school in such a house. In case of any violation of the provisions of this section, or of any failure to comply with, or of any violation of the terms and conditions of the plan for such tenement or lodging house approved by the department of buildings, or of the conditions of the permits granted as hereinbefore provided, or for the air, light and ventilation of the said house or premises, any court of record, or any judge or justice thereof, shall have power, at any time after service of notice of violation, or of non-compliance, upon the owner, builder, or other person superintending the building or converting any such house, upon proof by affidavit of any violation or non-compliance as aforesaid, or that a plan for light and ventilation of such house has not been approved by the department of buildings, to restrain by injunction order, in any action by the department of buildings, or by the board of health, the further progress of any violation as aforesaid. No undertaking shall be required as a condition of granting an injunction, or by reason thereof.

Dimensions and ventilation of rooms.—Sec. 1,319. In every such house hereafter erected or converted, every habitable room, except rooms in the attic, shall be in every part, not less than eight feet in height from the floor to the ceiling; and every habitable room in the attic

of any such building shall be at least eight feet in height
from the floor to the ceiling, throughout not less than one-
half the area of such room.   Every such room shall have at
least one window connecting with the external air, or over
the door a ventilator of perfect construction, connecting
it with a room or hall which has a connection with the external air, and so arranged as to produce a cross current
of air.   The total area of window or windows in every
room communicating with the external air shall be at
least one-tenth of the superficial area of every such room;
and the top of one, at least, of such windows, shall not be
less than seven feet six inches above the floor, and the
upper half, at least, shall be made so as to open the full
width.   Every habitable room of a less area than one hun=
dred superficial feet, if it does not communicate directly
with the external air, and is without an open fire-place,
shall be provided with special means of ventilation, by a
separate air shaft extending to the roof, or otherwise, as
the board of health may prescribe.

**Chimneys, ash receptacles, water, cellar floor, ceil-
ings and gas in tenement houses.**—Sec. 1,320.   Every
such house erected after May fourteenth, eighteen hundred
and sixty-seven, or converted, shall have adequate chimney
for a stove, properly connected with one of said chimneys
for every family set of apartments.   It shall have proper
conveniences and receptacles for ashes and rubbish.   It
shall have water furnished in sufficient quantity at one or
more places on each floor, occupied or intended to be occupied by one or more families; and all tenement houses
shall be provided with a like supply of water by the owners
thereof, whenever they shall be directed to do so by the
board of health.   But a failure in the general supply of
water by the city authorities, shall not be construed to be

a failure on the part of such owner, provided that proper and suitable appliances to receive and distribute such water are placed in said house. The board of health shall require all tenement houses to be so supplied. Every tenement house shall have the floor of the cellar made water tight; and the ceiling plastered, and when the house is located over filled in ground, or over marshy ground, or ground on which water lies, the cellar floor shall be covered so as to effectually prevent evaporation or dampness. It shall be the duty of the department of health to see that the cellars of all tenement houses are so made or altered as to comply with this section. Every such house erected after May seventh, eighteen hundred and eighty-seven, or converted, shall have the halls on each floor open directly to the external air, with suitable windows, and shall have no room or other obstruction at the end, unless sufficient light or ventilation is otherwise provided for in said halls, in a manner approved by the department of buildings. The owner or lessee of every tenement or lodging house in the city of New York shall keep a light burning in the hallway upon each floor of said house from sunset until 10 P. M. throughout the year. In every tenement house in the said city in which there is a hallway or hallways with no window opening from such hallway outside of said house, a light shall be maintained by said owner or lessee in each such hallway, between the hours of 8 A. M. and 10 P. M. of each day, unless said hallway shall be otherwise sufficiently lighted. The fire department of the city of New York is hereby vested with authority to prescribe reasonable regulations concerning such precautions as may be necessary to prevent danger from fire arising from such lights.

Overcrowding of tenement houses prohibited; house-

keeper in same required.—Sec. 1,321. Whenever it shall be certified to the department of health by the sanitary superintendent or an assistant sanitary superintendent that any tenement house or room therein, being without sufficient ventilation, is so overcrowded that there shall be afforded less than four hundred cubic feet of air to each adult, and two hundred cubic feet of air to each child under twelve years of age occupying such building or room, the said department shall issue an order requiring the number of occupants of such building, or room, to be reduced in accordance with this provision. Whenever there shall be more than eight families living in any tenement house, in which the owner thereof does not reside, there shall be a janitor, housekeeper or some other responsible person, who shall reside in the said house, and have charge of the same, if the department of health shall so require. Permits may be granted by the board of health to the owners of lodging houses on compliance with the rules and regulations of the sanitary code in the city of New York, and the conditions of each permit which shall be in writing.

The City Court of New York is continued in existence by section 1345. This is the old "Marine Court," of New York City, and is now continued *only in the territory of the old City*, as it existed prior to June 6th, 1895, (What is now the Borough of Manhattan). This omits all that was added on 6th June, 1895, viz.: parts of the towns of Westchester, Eastchester, Pelham ; that is, parts of the villages of Wakefield, Eastchester, and Williamsbridge. These were not under the jurisdiction of the City Court, and are not now.

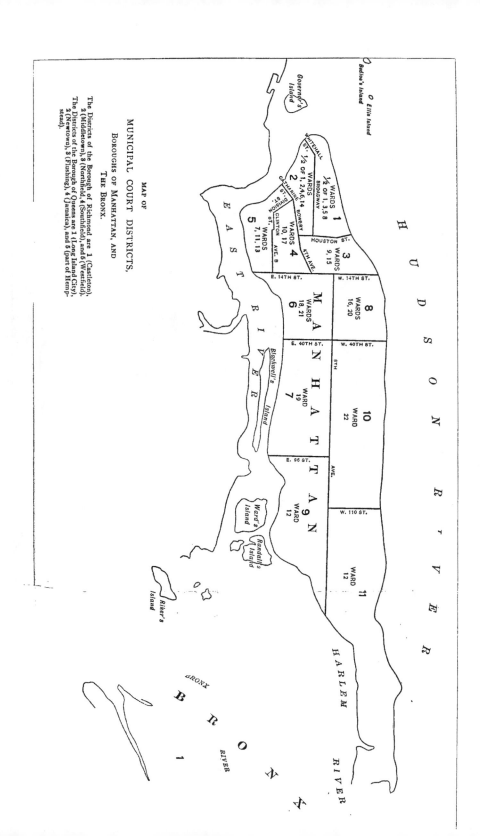

MAP OF
MUNICIPAL COURT DISTRICTS,
BOROUGHS OF MANHATTAN, AND
THE BRONX.

The Districts of the Borough of Richmond are 1 (Castleton), 2 (Middletown), 3 (Northfield, 4 (Southfield), and 6 (Westfield).
The Districts of the Borough of Queens are 1 (Long Island City), 2 (Newtown), 3 (Flushing), 4 (Jamaica), and 5 (part of Hempstead).

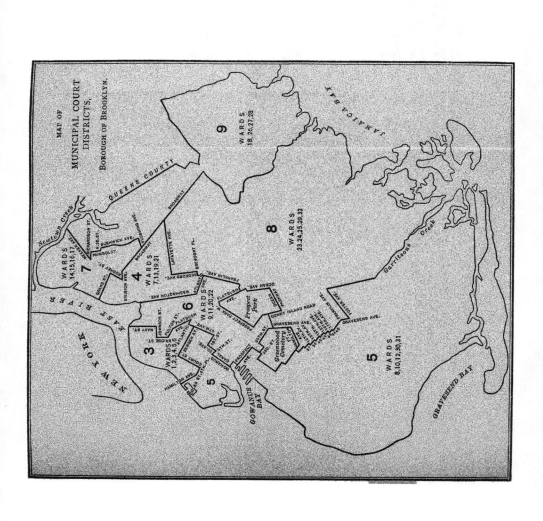

MAP OF
MUNICIPAL COURT
DISTRICTS,
BOROUGH OF BROOKLYN.

This seems to me a mistake. I think it would have been better to have enlarged the territory of its jurisdiction, so as to have covered all the Boroughs, the whole of the new City. But there would be the inconveniences of travel to overcome had that been done.

As far as real estate is concerned, the City Court never had, and has not now, jurisdiction over that, except in *dispossess proceedings* (the same as the district courts and justices of the peace) and in causes in which *title to land* comes in question (in the pleadings or in the course of the trial) ; [in district courts and courts of justices of the peace, when this happens—when a question of title arises —the judge has to dismiss the suit. This is because they are not courts *of record*, and have no equity powers].

District Courts are abolished in the old City of New York, **and** so are **justices of the peace** in **Brooklyn** and **Long Island City.** (Sec. 135ƒ.)

Justices of the Peace remain in Richmond County, and in the parts of Queens County included in the new City.

The Municipal Court is the name of the new court which takes the place of the old District Courts, etc.— "The Municipal Court of the City of New York." There are to be twenty-three of these courts, or, rather, twenty-three districts, in each of which sessions of this court are to be held.

Borough of The Bronx.—Sec. 1,359. In the borough of The Bronx there shall be two districts, as follows:

1. The first district embracing the territory described in

6

chapter 934 of the laws of 1895.   That is the towns of West-chester, Eastchester and Pelham, being parts of the villages of Wakefield, Eastchester, and Williamsbridge.

2. The second district embracing the remainder of said borough.

Borough of Manhattan.—Sec. 1,360.   In the borough of Manhattan there shall be eleven districts, as follows:

1. The First district embraces the Third, Fifth and Eighth wards of said borough of Manhattan, and all that part of the First ward lying west of Broadway and Whitehall street, including Nuttin or Governor's Island, Bedloe's Island, Bucking or Ellis Island and the Oyster islands.

2. The Second embraces the Second, Fourth, Sixth and Fourteenth wards, and all that portion of the First ward lying south and east of Broadway and Whitehall street.

3. The Third district embraces the Ninth and Fifteenth wards.

4. The Fourth district embraces the Tenth and Seventeenth wards.

5. The Fifth district embraces the Seventh, Eleventh and Thirteenth wards.

6. The Sixth district embraces the Eighteenth and Twenty-first wards.

7. The Seventh district embraces the Nineteenth ward.

8. The Eighth district embraces the Sixteenth and Twentieth wards.

9. The Ninth district embraces the Twelfth ward, except that portion thereof which lies west of the center line of Lenox or Sixth avenue and of the Harlem river north of the terminus of Lenox avenue.

10. The Tenth district embraces the Twenty-second ward and all that portion of the Twelfth ward which is bounded

on the north by the center line of One Hundred and Tenth street, on the south by the center line of Eighty-sixth street, on the east by the center line of Sixth avenue and on the west by the North river.

11. The Eleventh district embraces that portion of the Twelfth ward which lies north of the center line of West One Hundred and Tenth street and west of the center line of Lenox or Sixth avenue and of the Harlem river north of the terminus of Lenox or Sixth avenue.

Borough of Brooklyn.—Sec. 1,361. In the borough of Brooklyn there shall be five districts as follows:

1. The First district embraces the First, Second, Third, Fourth, Fifth, Sixth, Tenth and Twelfth wards.

2. The Second district embraces the Seventh, Eighth, Ninth, Eleventh, Twentieth, Twenty-first, Twenty-second and Twenty-third wards.

3. The Third district embraces the Thirteenth, Fourteenth, Fifteenth, Sixteenth, Seventeenth, Eighteenth and Nineteenth wards.

4. The Fourth district embraces the Twenty-fourth, Twenty-fifth, Twenty-sixth, Twenty-seventh and Twenty-eighth wards.

5. The Fifth district embraces the Twenty-ninth, Thirtieth, Thirty-first and Thirty-second wards.

Borough of Queens.—Sec. 1,362. In the borough of Queens there shall be three districts, as follows:

1. The First district embraces Ward One of said borough. (Long Island City.)

2. The Second district embraces Wards Two and Three of said borough. (Newtown and Flushing.)

3. The Third district embraces Wards Four and Five of said borough. (Jamaica and part of Hempstead.)

Borough of Richmond.—Sec. 1,363. In the borough of Richmond there shall be two districts, as follows:

1. The First district embraces Wards One and Three of said borough. (Castleton and Northfield.)

2. The Second district embraces Wards, Two, Four and Five of said borough. (Middletown, Southfield and Westfield.)

Dispossess or Summary Proceedings are to be brought in these municipal courts, each case in the court within whose district the real estate or a part of it is situated.

These Courts have jurisdiction in various other matters also. (Sec. 1364.)

But they can *not* take cognizance of any civil action where the title to real property comes in question (except in dispossess proceedings aforesaid). (Sec. 1365.) And if the question of title does not appear in the complaint, the defendant can make an affidavit that it will come up in the answer and can give a bond and remove it to the Supreme Court.

These Courts are where the suits will be tried for the recovery of fines and penalties against you for breaking the rules, known or unknown, of the Board of Health, and of the Building Department, and of the Street Cleaning Department, and for breaches of other ordinances and rules. (Sec. 1370, Subdivision 5.)

The Location of each of these Municipal District Courts is to be named by the Municipal Assembly within 30 days after December 31st, 1897. (Sec. 1371.)

The rules of the Code of Civil Procedure relating to contempt of Court apply to this Municipal Court, except that a Judge of this Court can not be punished for contempt for not proceeding with a suit. And a jury must always be twelve men, not six.

Times and Places and Hours of holding these Municipal District Courts are to be adopted by the board of all the justices of these courts, before January 25th, and are to be published in the City Record, and in one newspaper *published in each* Borough, before February 1st. (Sec. 1375.) So you will know where to go for dispossess proceedings.

All suits pending in the District Courts and before justices of the peace, on January 31st, 1898, are to be adjourned over to the Municipal District Court of their respective districts, to February 1st, 1898, or some day following. (Sec. 1382.)

The Acquisition of Land for public purposes is governed by sections 1435 to 1448. As your interests in any such proceedings require that you should retain a lawyer to protect them, it is unnecessary to analyze all those details in this hand-book intended for laymen. These sections, 1435 to 1447, apply to acquisition of land by the City for every purpose *except* for streets, avenues, parks, water supply and wharves. (Sec. 1448.)

Maps or plans have to be prepared (and the agents of the City are authorized to enter anywhere and everywhere in the daytime to make surveys for such maps or plans) Three Commissioners of Estimate have to be appointed in each case by the Supreme Court after ten days' notice published in the City Record; these commissioners have to report to the court and the court can confirm it, or refer it back again for modification, and thereafter confirm it.

The City at once **becomes the owner,** "seized in fee simple absolute," on the final confirmation of the report.

The City may at once **enter into possession** of the property, upon that final confirmation of the report, *without paying a cent.*

All co**venants, contracts or engagements between landlords and tenants** (or any other parties) relating to that property shall, upon confirmation of such report, *cease and determine and be absolutely discharged* according to law. (Sec. 1438.)

Title may be vested in the City before confirmation by the Court if the Department or Board that wants the land feels in a hurry, and passes a resolution which states that they want title to vest in the City four months from the date of the filing of the oaths of the Commissioners of Estimate. But in this case interest on the amount afterwards awarded to the owners is to begin to run in their favor from that date (four months after the filing of the commissioner's oaths); and all leases and contracts about that land cease and determine, and are discharged on that date (when title vests in the City.) (Sec. 1439.)

These Commissioners of Estimate have to deposit their report in the office of the Department or Board which is conducting the proceeding, and give fifteen days' notice in the "City Record" of its presentation for confirmation, at which time objections may be made to it.

The City shall pay for the land taken within ten months after confirmation of the report, or from the day the title vested if that was fixed by the department wanting it, under section 1438. Interest begins to run against the City at the end of that ten months (in addition to the interest allowed by section 1439, when the land has been taken under section 1438.)   (Sec. 1440.)

Owners who are Unknown, or who are Infants, or of Unsound Mind, are protected by the provisions of section 1441.

Appeal may be taken within twenty days after notice of the confirmation of the report, by any party who feels aggrieved. (Sec. 1442.)   But such an appeal will not stay the proceedings, except only as to the particular piece of property with which the appeal is concerned.

In case of death, resignation, insanity, disqualification, refusal or neglect to act, or of removal of any such commissioner, the Court can appoint a new one, under section 1443.

The Powers of the Commissioners, and their Fees and Expenses, are provided for by section 1444.

Amendments of Defects or informalities may be made by the Court at any time, on such notice as it deems proper. (Sec. 1445.)

A Commissioner may be removed by the Court, in its judgment, at any time. (Sec. 1445.)

The Corporation Counsel must appear and protect the City in all such proceedings. (Sec. 1446.)

The Source of Payment of Awards and Expenses is stated and detailed in section 1447.

The use of the streets by foot-passengers, vehicles and animals is to be governed and regulated by ordinances to be passed by the Municipal Assembly. And until new ordinances are passed, the laws and ordinances now applicable in the different parts of the new city are to govern. (Sec. 1,454.)

There are over 1,100 miles of paved streets and several hundred more of unpaved streets in Greater New York.

Law of the Road is "Keep to the right." Sec. 1,455. And another rule of the road is that if you pass a vehicle going the same way, you should pass it on the left side. Friends in the rural districts can often tell a "Yorker" from his disregard of this rule; he will so often try to drive past another wagon on the right side instead of on the left as he ought. This is also the correct rule for *foot* passengers meeting, "Keep to the right." It is noticeable, however, that great numbers of people stick to the old *English* rule:

"The rule of the road is a paradox quite,
    When you go right you go wrong, and when
        you go left you go right."

Don't let your servant or employe throw any ashes, garbage, dirt or paper in the street, or you'll be liable to ten dollars or ten days.

So, too, if you or your employe should leave a wagon or

cart, unharnessed, upon any street, or any box or barrel or bale of merchandise upon the sidewalk. Sec. 1,456.

License for Amusements or Public Exhibitions. If you lease or let your building, or part of your building, to be used for any theatrical performance, or amusement, or for acrobats, etc., or if you consent to your tenant's using the premises for any such purpose, without such license having been *previously* obtained, you are liable to $100 fine. (Sec. 1,473.) Fortunately this does not apply to private theatricals and the exhibitions given for charitable, religious, masonic, or educational purposes. (Sec. 1,480.)

The "City Record," the official journal of the City of New York, is to be published daily (Sundays and legal holidays excepted). It is to be controlled by a board composed of the Mayor, Corporation Counsel, and Comptroller, who appoint the manager called the Supervisor of the City Record. (Sec. 1,526.)

Barber shops may be open on Sunday until one o'clock in the afternoon hereafter, in all of the territory of the City of New York as they have been permitted since 1895 in the old city. (Sec. 1,535.)

The Territory of Grants and Franchises is not extended to cover the territory of the new City, however, where such franchises and grants were given originally for the territory of the old city. (Sec. 1,538.)

Nor is the Price of Gas in Richmond and Queens counties affected by this Charter.

Dedication of Streets and Highways to the Public will

not become effectual or binding hereafter until the map or plot has been submitted by the owner and approved by the Board of Public Improvements. But upon such approval the title of the owners to all streets, avenues and public places designated on such map or plot will immediately vest in fee clear of all incumbrances in the City of New York, in trust for the designated uses. (Sec. 1,540.)

A Quorum of a Board in any Department of the city government, and also of the Board or the Revision of Assessments, is a majority of the members of the Board. (Sec. 1541.)

All City Real Estate sold must be sold at auction (except land under water). (Sec. 1553.)

The Wards of Brooklyn are to continue with the boundaries and numbers to be the Wards of the Borough of Brooklyn. (Sec. 1577.)

The Wards of old New York and North of the Harlem River continue with their boundaries and numbers to be the Wards of the Boroughs of Manhattan and The Bronx, respectively. (Sec. 1578.)

Towns and Villages in Richmond County, the five towns and all the villages, are *abolished*. (Sec. 1579.)

The Wards in the Borough of Richmond, are : One (old town of Castleton), Two (old Middletown), Three (old Northfield), Four (old Southfield), and Five (old Westfield). (Sec. 1580.)

Towns and Villages in Queens County; the three towns, and all the villages in the part added to Greater New York, are abolished. (Sec. 1581.)

The Wards in the Borough of Queens, are: One (Long Island City), Two (the former town of Newtown), Three (the old town of Flushing), Four (the old town of Jamaica), and Five (that *part* of the town of Hempstead included in the new City, The City of New York.)

But the **Supervisors** of those towns in office January 1st, 1898, are to serve out their respective terms as supervisors and as members of the Board of Supervisors of Queens County. (Section 1581.)

Bear in mind that the old *towns* of Flushing, Newtown and Jamaica are respectively larger than the old *villages* of the same name.

Boundaries of the Wards may be changed, and **new** Wards may be created hereafter by the Municipal Assembly. (Sec. 1582.)

The Proportion of the Debts of Queens County and of the Town of Hempstead that are to be assumed by the new City, are to be determined under the provisions of section 1588 and section 1589, respectively ; and the apportionment of the amounts of State taxes and of the school moneys, for each of the Counties consolidated, are to be determined under sections 1593 to 1597.

Old Franchises and Grants are not affected by this new charter, but the grants of franchises or properties or rights of any nature, in, to or concerning property of any character, or other grants made by the Nicoll's charter, the Dongan charter, the Cornbury charter, the Montgomerie charter, by the Confirmation Act, passed October 14,

1732, or by any other Act or charter granted by the State of New York, to the cities, municipalities and public corporations consolidated by this new charter, are ratified, granted, confirmed and extended to the City of New York, as constituted by this Act. (Sec. 1617.)

A huge Machine.—The careful study which I have been obliged to give to this new Charter, in order to write this monograph upon its Bearing upon Real Estate Interests, has impressed me with the comprehensive, broad, and thorough manner in which the Charter has been drafted, following a well-defined plan, and with an eye to every detail, forgetting nothing necessary, deftly fitting all parts together, it is a monument to the ability of the man who drafted it, and of the men who may have amended it into its final shape.

But it is an instrument of despotic power. As a citizen whose family has been identified with the City since its settlement, in A. D. 1623, as an American conscious of his own rights, and with a regard for the rights of others, I look forward to the effects and results of this one-man power, wielding the power of an irresponsible majority, with the gravest anxiety for individual rights and for civic honor. This Charter will not work by the power of the people governing the Mayor. Some party bound together for spoils will elect the Mayor, and will perpetuate itself : it is too much to expect anything else from human nature.

And Real Estate will foot the bills.

GEO. W. VAN SICLEN.

ANALYTICAL INDEX

By GEO. W. VAN SICLEN.

GUIDE TO BUYERS AND SELLERS OF REAL ESTATE

HOW TO DRAW A CONTRACT

BY

GEO. W. VAN SICLEN

Counsellor at Law.

TOGETHER WITH

THE REAL PROPERTY LAW

Of the State of New York of October 1, 1896,

INDEXED.

REAL ESTATE RECORD AND GUIDE,

PUBLISHERS,

14–16 VESEY ST., NEW YORK.

165 pages. Price, $1.00 in cloth; 75 cents in paper.

THE STANDARD AUTHORITY.

LAWS RELATING TO BUILDING
IN NEW YORK CITY,

(With the New Charter Amendments,)

BY

WILLIAM J. FRYER,
Member of the Board of Examiners.

A volume of 450 pages, containing all the laws that have any direct bearing upon Building operations; illustrated, indexed and furnished with marginal notes. This is the only *complete* work for the Architect, Engineer, Builder and Real Estate Owner. It contains the Building Law; Law Limiting the Height of Dwelling Houses; Plumbing, Elevator, Light and Ventilation, Electric Light, Power and Heat Regulations; Tenement and Lodgiug House Laws; Regulations of the Department of Public Works; Police Department rules concerning buildings, Inspection of Steam Boilers; Laws Relating to the Extinction and Prevention of Fires; a Directory of Architects, etc., etc.

Price, in cloth, - = $2.50.

RECORD AND GUIDE, 14–16 VESEY STREET,
NEW YORK CITY.

THE INVESTOR'S PAPER.

The Record and Guide

(Established 1868.)

A WEEKLY JOURNAL THAT WILL

MAKE MONEY

FOR

The Real Estate Investor,

The Real Estate Owner,

The Real Estate Broker and Auctioneer,

The Building Material Dealer,

The Real Estate Lawyer,

The Architect,

The Builder,

And All Who Give Credit,

The Banker, Brewer, Furniture Dealer and General Merchant.

**Send to the Office of Publication,
14-16 Vesey Street; New York City,
For a Sample Copy . . . . . .**

FRANCIS T. UNDERHILL,

Real Estate,

9 PINE STREET,   NEW YORK.
(Ground Floor.)

Telephone Call, 4786 Cortlandt.

GERMAN-AMERICAN
REAL ESTATE TITLE
———————GUARANTEE CO.,

36 Nassau Street, New York.
MUTUAL LIFE INS. CO. BUILDING,

TELEPHONE:
No. 1464 CORTLANDT, N. Y.
No. 1316 BROOKLYN.

BROOKLYN OFFICE,
40 COURT STREET.

CASH CAPITAL, $500,000.

This Company affords absolute protection to purchasers of Real Estate.

TITLES EXAMINED AND GUARANTEED.

MONEY LOANED ON BOND AND MORTGAGE.

EDWARD V. LOEW, President.
GEORGE C. CLAUSEN, Vice-President.
C. J. OBERMAYER, Sec'y and Treas.
CHARLES UNANGST, Counsel.
HON. NOAH DAVIS, Advisory Counsel.

DIRECTORS.

SILAS B. DUTCHER,	GEORGE C. CLAUSEN,
GEORGE W. QUINTARD,	RUSSELL SAGE,
EDWARD V. LOEW,	WILLIAM WAGNER,
JAMES FELLOWS,	JOSEPH J. KITTEL,
DAVID H. McALPIN,	JOHN WEBER,
EDWARD UHL,	JUNIUS N. PETTY,
C. J. OBERMAYER,	GEORGE H. BEYER,
FRANK M. WEILER,	EDWARD M. BURGHART,
JOHN GUTH,	FREDERICK G. YUENGLING,
VAN MATER STILLWELL,	CHARLES UNANGST.